Tr

The other day I realized, as a cold claw of pure fear squeezed my frantic heart, that I have been working as a video clerk for ten months.

This is a job that I took on a temporary basis for just a month or two until freelancing picked back up and I got my finances in order.

Ten months.

It has been a test of patience, humility, and character.

It has been a lesson in dealing with all humankind, including their personal bodily fluids.

It has been $6.50 an hour.

Tae Bo

A guy came up to the counter a few days ago and asked me if *Tae Bo* was in.

I explained that we don't carry exercise videos and he said no, we had it – he'd seen the box downstairs. Downstairs is, of course, the porn section.

Some porn movies do ape mainstream titles – *David Cop-a-Feel* was my all-time favorite – but not as many as you'd think. A lot just follow a simple pattern: (A) B N, where A is the race of the participants (optional), B is the sex act or kink – sometimes this gets astonishingly specific – and N is the number of the series. Thus, you get *Blow Bang 25* or *Asian All-Anal Action 15*.

The *Little White Chicks, Big Black Monster Dicks* series (note intriguing combination of race and fetish) has some of the most offensive cover art I've ever seen, not because of the sexual content but because it's incredibly racist. The little white chicks look at you demurely over their shoulders while surrounded by scowling African-American men. The men are repeatedly referred to as "monsters" ("monster dicks" itself doesn't bother me because it merely implies that said dicks are monstrously large, but referring to the men themselves as monsters is another story) and their faces are actually mounted on cartoon animal bodies. There's no way in hell you could put that cover on, say, a book and not get your store burnt down, and perhaps rightly so. But my well-intentioned liberalism can pretty much go screw itself, because the series is cheerfully (and heavily) rented by people of all races.

Anyway, *Tae Bo*. I can't find it in the computer, but that's not unusual – deliberate misspellings are common in porn. That, plus the inevitable similarity of titles makes it a real pain in the butt to look things up. Does the customer want *Black Ball*, *Blackball*, *Black Balled*, *Blackballed*, *Black Balls*, *Blackballs*, *Black Ballers*, *BlackBallers*, *Black Ballz*, *Blackballz*, *Black Ballerz*, or *BlackBallerz*? And does he want the one in the gay section or the one in the straight section?

But I keep looking. The Zen lesson of my job is this: just because I do not want to be a video clerk doesn't mean I shouldn't be the best possible video clerk I can be. There's no way to just pop up a partial alphabetical list of titles, so you have to pick a likely starting point and then flip through entry after entry.

"It was a weird spelling, right?" I ask, still typing in variations on *Tae Bo* as fast as I can think of them.

"Yes," he says "It was spelled weird."

"Do you remember it?"

Yes, he does: T-A-B-O-O

Lube Warning

We all abuse the hand sanitizer. We can't help it.

Contamination is everywhere. I see people sneezing onto the tape cases. They cough wetly into their palms right before handing me change. They squeegee out their ears with their pinkies. They forget about the security cameras downstairs and pick their noses with wild abandon and astonishing force. Still, the only thing that really freaks me out is the semen. Well, OK, the lubricant freaks me out too, but I'm pretty sure that's because of the implied presence of semen.

The only thing we can do is use the hand sanitizer. I use it so much that I lose all finger traction and can't open our plastic bags. I've had days when I've used it so much that I can't make fingerprints on the glass countertop. It freaks me out, but the thought of not using it is worse.

Sometimes people get animalistic about the tapes. For the real addicts (I'm convinced that porn is like alcohol: some people can stop at just one every now and then, some people just binge on weekends, and some people get genuinely, horribly addicted) the reptilian brain kicks in. They hit the magic portion of the tape and they're done. They pop out the tape and slam in another one, and the next day the stack comes back, unrewound and covered in goo.

Repeat offenders get a note on their files that says "LUBE WARNING". Management policy is that for $6.50 an hour, clerks should not have to deal with the bodily fluids of others. The first time we discreetly but firmly remind the customer that the tapes need to come back clean. The second time we hand him the tape, the Windex, and the paper towels and tell him to clean off the tape in full view of whoever else is at the counter.

It astonishes me that someone could actually forget to clean off his sticky and/or slippery tapes, but what amazes me even more is that people actually have the balls to argue with us about it. They always claim they got the tapes that way. They will actually claim that the spooge in question was missed by both the clerk that checked it in and the clerk that checked it back out, and that they figured what the hell, they'd go ahead and play it, even though it was covered in gel.

One guy brought back a DVD with a big white thumbprint of come on it. He actually tried to argue with me: "That's not mine. I never even played that! I never even took it out of the case!"

I pointed out that the disc had been put back in the case with the reverse side up, which was where the thumbprint was. The clerk couldn't have checked the movie out to him that way because the serial number is on the front. The guy still tried to protest that sure, maybe he'd picked it up and looked at it but –

"Sir," I said, "It's your thumbprint. Do you really want to get into this?"

He did not.

I hate it when people argue, but I understand why they do. I don't think there should be any shame in masturbating, but I do think there should be shame in expecting someone with whom you are not very, very close to deal with a wad of your spooge. I think they get all defensive because in that moment, they realize it too. But I think there's more to it than that.

One of my favorite concepts in anthropology is that of the polite fiction. It's something nobody believes, but we all pretend to because it makes life so much easier. My favorite example was of a Pygmy couple. Pygmy divorce involves quite literally breaking up the home: the couple tears apart their house (it's easy – the roofs are made of leaves) and once it's down, the union is dissolved. One anthropologist was watching a long-married couple have a fight. It escalated until the wife threatened to leave, and the husband yelled something along the lines of "Fine!" and there was nothing the wife could do but start tearing down the house. She began tearing the roof off, clearly miserable. The husband looked wretched too, but at this point neither could back down without losing face and by now the whole village was watching.

Finally, the husband called out the Pygmy equivalent of "You're right, honey! The roof is dirty! It'll look much better once we get those leaves washed!" The two of them started carrying leaves down to the river, soon with the help of the whole village, and then washed and rebuilt the roof. When the anthropologist later discreetly asked how often one washes the roof, everyone looked at him like he was a complete doofus.

The polite fiction of the porn section is that, while people do generally use porn for the purpose of masturbation, there is no reason to believe that this particular customer will be doing so. He could be using them for his Master's thesis. Hell, he may not get around to watching them at all. We all like to believe that. When it becomes all too clear to everyone involved that said customer did, in fact, not only lube up, watch the tape, stroke himself to orgasm, and then grab the damned thing without even taking the basic courtesy of washing his goddamned hands first, we all get uncomfortable.

On the other hand, he gets angry because he's ashamed of something that was entirely avoidable and his own fault. I'm supposed to keep my temper even though I've just put my hand in a wad of his semen.

The destruction of the polite fiction is what creeps me out about one of my weekend regulars. He comes in when I open at nine, then chooses and rents two movies. He leaves for exactly two movies' worth of time, then returns them before four to get the matinee special. I hate it because there's no way to pretend he's been doing anything else. I just hope to God there's been a hand washing between him and me. I think there is, because his tapes are always clean, but it still gives me the shivers and sends me straight to the hand sanitizer. It's just too much to know.

Mr. Glasses is the very creepiest, though. He's always very friendly, even courtly. He's too friendly, actually – he's always doing stuff like announcing "It's THAT kind of personal service that sets your store apart from the Blockbusters!" Yeah, whatever. The over-friendliness itself is creepy, as is the way he sort of doesn't blink enough and doesn't know that most business transactions don't really involve sustained eye contact. (No, he's not hitting on me. He's gay.) But of course what puts him over the top is that he's our biggest repeat lube offender. I hate seeing him coming. It's like Russian Roulette.

Rainy days are the worst. He just plunks a wet bag on the counter and we have to reach in and get the tapes. You know that initiation ritual in *Flash Gordon* where the guy has to stick his hand way, way down a hole and usually it's fine but sometimes there's a venomous beastie at the end that stings him? It's like that.

Actually, it isn't quite. The tapes are always a bit wet on rainy days – it's just that my brain can't stop churning about what they might be wet with.

We all abuse the hand sanitizer. And I am deeply grateful that it exists.

Customers I Have Driven out of the Store

If you don't count rousting teenagers out of the porn section, I have only driven away two and a half customers.

The only one I'm proud of happened pretty recently. I was ringing up a sale and I heard a crash from downstairs. My manager was out, so I couldn't leave the register to go down and see what happened. I glanced at the security monitor and saw a guy downstairs calmly flipping through the DVD section. He had knocked down three entire shelves. Instead of picking them up or coming to get me or even shoving them over into a pile and then continuing his porn shopping, he was just standing in them and on them, flipping away.

I got on the Voice of God microphone and said, in as friendly a voice as I could, "Hi! Could you pick those up, please?"

He started, then came charging up the stairs. "It was an accident!" he yelled, "Knocking over those DVDs was an accident!"

"I believe you, sir." I said.

"And you want me to pick them up? You want ME to pick them up?!"

And without waiting for an answer, he stormed out.

I didn't really expect him to pick them up. I wouldn't have minded picking them up if he'd just come upstairs and said something like "Jesus, I'm an idiot and I knocked down a substantial chunk of your DVD section." Or put them into halfhearted little piles. Or really anything other than just standing on them while continuing to shop for porn.

I don't think he was as angry at the notion that he might have to clean up his own mess so much as he was furious that he'd been caught making it. Sometimes new customers don't see the security cameras right away, and they sure as hell don't expect the Voice of God mic. When you're scrutinizing the charming cover art of *White Trash Whore*, the last thing you want is to be chastised by a booming voice from above.

I'm not particularly sorry we lost his business. I do feel bad about driving away Mr. Creaky, even though he used to give me the creeps. Mr. Creaky was not, technically, a porn customer. He liked the Japanese animation. The Anime section is the one that really makes me cringe. It's upstairs in the general releases since it's all, you know, cartoons. Some of it is charming fare like *My Neighbor Totoro*, but a lot of it is incredibly hardcore stuff – way worse than we allow in the real-people porn downstairs.

My position on porn is that I'm fine with whatever floats your boat, as long as everyone involved is a consenting adult. Hentai throws both parts of that rule out the window. Sure, all the boxes claim that all the characters are at least 18, but a lot of them are drawn to look about 12. And there's a lot of raping. Not just run-of-the-mill raping, either – we're talking about triple-penetration rape by demons.

I consider myself a first-amendment feminist, but to be honest the hentai really makes me wrestle with that sometimes. And guys who rent the entire *La Blue Girl* series all at once (check out the box cover sometime and you'll see what I mean) freak me out even worse than the guys who rent the *Animal Trainer* series.[1]

We have to watch the Anime section because it's right next to the foreign films and the tags are the same color, which means a clerk who isn't on his toes could check out a shitload of hardcore animated underage rape porn to a kid and yes, once they see that there's sex stuff on some of the boxes kids definitely try to slide it past.

Mr. Creaky, as you've guessed, was hardly a kid. I would have been frightened of him if he hadn't been so old and feeble. He would rent a stack of rape hentai at least once a week. He always had the same patter as he came up to the register:

"Do you watch that show *The Sopranos*?"

"No, sir."

"I hear it's pretty good."

"Yes, sir, that's what I hear too."

---

[1] No, we don't carry bestiality. *Animal Trainer* is about training women.

"I'd like to watch that show, but I can't. There's too much cussing."

Then, clever ruse in place, he would bring up his tags for *Demon Beast*.

Anyway, all would have been well had it not been for a well meaning but plateheaded clerk name Dan. Dan was a sweetheart, but had an astonishing ability to fuck things up. In this case, Dan had rented six of our very foulest titles to a 16-year-old. To give you the idea of the level of stupidity this involves, I'll just go ahead and tell you that the *La Blue Girl* series depicts a woman being raped by demons RIGHT ON THE BOX. I was horrified both at the thought of what this kid's mom would do to us when she found out and what the kid himself had just learned about the beautiful, tender world of lovemaking.

I talked to my manager. We didn't want to move the whole Anime section, so we needed a bright, easy signal for Dan, who for some reason still hadn't been fired. Our solution was to let the R-rated stuff slide, but if anything looked more like an X I highlighted the label on the tag and wrote a big "NC-17" on it.[2]

Mr. Creaky never came back.

So how did I manage to drive away half a customer? Well, he's not really quite gone yet. He still comes into the store a lot, but I may have destroyed his soul.

---

[2] Yes, this was a violation of MPAA copyright.

Mr. Buddy was the first guy people warned me about when I started working at the store.

He is heavily addicted to porn and a huge pain in the ass. He also desperately wants to be friends with the clerks. He wants to come behind the counter and look at the boxes when new porn comes in. We always tell him that customers can't come behind the counter and he says, "Yeah, but I can, right?" No, he can't. Sometimes with a new clerk he'll try "The old manager used to let me come behind the counter," at which point any other employee in earshot will chime in with "No, he didn't." He bitches about the prices and tries to haggle with us. "I swear to you, this has been on the new release shelf for a long time. I should get it for the old release price, right?" Wrong.

One time he brought back just a case, without the DVD in it. He actually expected me to check the empty case in and let him, you know, just drop the DVD by at his convenience. When I said no, he stood at the register and whined for nearly ten minutes.

His bitching and wheedling isn't caused so much by the fact that he's a cheapskate, which he is, as by the fact that he desperately wants to be a regular. He wants to be greeted by name and not have to show ID and get whatever mythical special privileges he's imagining. The problem, of course, is that we're the ones who decide if he's a regular or not, and we don't like him.

The fact that he's an asshole is part of the problem, and the other part is that he seems to be completely devoid of social skills. Even the total dirtbags know better than to hit on me when I'm putting tags away downstairs. Mr. Buddy did not.

And again, he desperately, desperately wants to be friends with us. He's maybe 45 years old, and has a good enough job to spend literally thousands of dollars a year on porn. We can't figure out why he wants to be friends so badly, but he does. "You guys are awesome!" he'll say after trying to get Dustin to pay the extra $.50 he owes for him, "Seriously, you guys are the best!" Never, not once, has he received a positive response to this behavior, but he still does it. "You guys rule, you know that?" I've met golden retriever puppies with more dignity.

I always try to be civil to him in a distant, customer service sort of way, which is apparently the best he gets. ("You're always so nice to me! You rule!")

Round about September 14th, 2001, he brought in a picture he'd downloaded from the Internet. It was President Bush photoshopped so that he had a long beard and was dressed in vaguely Middle Eastern clothes. Mr. Buddy had drawn a cartoon voice balloon coming out of Bush's mouth so that he was saying, "Rent at [My Store's Name] Video!"

I wasn't offended so much by any sort of tastelessness as I was by the completely failed attempt at humor. There wasn't even a vestigial joke. Mr. Buddy handed it to me, I made the same noncommittal friendly noise you make when you've been handed a drawing by a small child, and then tried to hand it back. "No," he said, "I made it for you guys! You keep it!" So I kept it until he left, then threw it away. The next time Mr. Buddy came in he was all upset – he'd actually expected us to post it behind the register.

You wouldn't think it would be possible to drive away Mr. Buddy, but it turns out you can. As I said, I have always been civil with him, even when he is making yet another attempt to get me to waive his late fees. But a couple of weeks ago he caught me at the end of a heavy dirtball day.

We'd been swamped: pervs, box thieves, scam artists, people dropping tapes and running without paying for them, and plenty of general crabbiness. And it was a New Porn Day, so the phone had been ringing off the hook and I just wanted to get the hell out of there. I was very, very tired. Mr. Buddy was one of my last customers. He pulled his usual asshole routine for about five minutes, and then as I started checking out his tapes he launched into how awesome we were.

I don't remember the exact phrasing of what was said. I just remember that one of the other clerks made a joke about closing early or closing altogether, and Mr. Buddy said something like "Aw, you can't do that – I need you guys! Who am I gonna hang out with?"

"Oh, Jesus, don't say that!" I said, "We can't be your only source of emotional support!"

I tried to turn my voice up into a joke at the last second, which almost worked.

"Don't say that," Mr. Buddy tried to joke back, "You make me sound pathetic."

We made eye contact before I could compose my face. In that moment, Mr. Buddy knew that I do, in fact, find him pathetic. And I'm the nice one. He still comes in, but he isn't chatty anymore.

The other clerks love it. I feel like a creep.

I Hate Mr. Pig.

There are many customers that bug me, and quite a few that give me the willies. One or two set off a very primal alarm in my fear center, right in my gut. They make the hairs on the back of my neck stand up and I know, on a purely instinctual level, that they are very, very dangerous.

But the only one I really hate is Mr. Pig. I loathe Mr. Pig. I hate him so much I need a new word for it.

Mr. Pig is the first customer to win a snotty note on his file from me. I refrained from the sport of snotty customer file notes for months. Most of the time it's a genuine warning ("This guy might be moving pricing stickers" "WATCH OUT FOR JIZZ-MASTER ZERO"), but sometimes it's just us blowing off steam or trying to crack each other up. My favorite is "Mr. Excitement!!!!!!!!!!" on the file of the guy who seems to be part tree sloth, while others favor "Engage, Number One!" on the file of the guy who looks a little too much like Johnathan Frakes.

Funny, yes, but unprofessional. I held off until I ran into Mr. Pig. He came up to the counter with his briefcase and two or three designer shopping bags. The counter is designed for two customers, but he piled all his stuff across it to take up the whole space. He pulled his videos out of his bags, handed me the new tags he wanted to check out, and then whipped out his cell phone to make a call.

I have to check an ID when someone rents new videos and, of course, get them to pay for their returns. Mr. Pig took up the whole counter and made me wait through his entire conversation – about a very, very big deal and conducted at about 30,000 decibels – before I could do either. When he finally got off, he said "Sorry, I had to do that. It was a big deal," just in case I'd missed that point.

Yes, important enough to hold up me and a line, but not so urgent as to, say, start the conversation before he came in.

Finally, stack of porn in hand, Mr. Pig pulled his briefcase and designer bags – did I mention they were designer bags? Because he did. – off the counter and left, and thus became the recipient of my first snotty note: "THIS MAN WANTS YOU TO KNOW THAT HE IS VERY, VERY IMPORTANT."

That was all I noticed about him the first time. Over time, though, he has burned himself into my brain. He always takes up the whole counter no matter who else is waiting, he usually shouts into his cell phone, and he always makes sure to allude to how very important he is. He has a password on his account, "KITTY". It's an old, old policy that a few old customers still use, but at least they're not freaks about it. The idea is that if you don't have ID, you can just give your password. We don't do it anymore, but we let old customers keep them. Mr. Pig is very, very proud of having a password. When we ask for ID, he shouts that he has a password, then leans in very close so the riffraff can't hear and whispers "Kitty".

I always ask him for his ID anyway. It drives him nuts. He wants to be a regular even more than Mr. Buddy does, and he hates it when I ask to see ID. He talks about the old managers, the old policies, and how long he's been here. Then I ask to see his ID. Sometimes I wonder if he leaves the store and bursts into tears.

So far, all of this is pathetic. Who the hell is that invested in impressing his video clerk? I should be unable to summon up an ounce of human feeling for Mr. Pig at all beyond pity. But no, it's a deep, burning antagonism.

It's the punch cards that got me. We give all our customers a gold punch card each month. Each time they return a movie, they get a punch. After six punches, they get a free rental. After another six, they get half off, then a free again. There are about 30 spaces. Some of the heavy porn renters make it through a few cards a month, so it's not unusual to give out a new card before the month is over.

Mr. Pig figured out that two frees in a row is better than a free and a half off, so he gets his free punch and then asks for a new card. So he's screwing the store out of $1.75 twice a month. Fine. It would be one thing if he just asked for his goddamned new card each time, but he can't just leave it at that. He's so proud of his penny-ante fucking over the store that he has to make a big deal out of it. "For heaven's sake," he'll bellow, "Can I PLEASE have a new card?" And then he won't quite have his old not-fully-punched card out of sight, in the hopes that the clerk will call him on it so he can launch into his speech about how very clever he is.

I just want him to know that I am not impressed. I want him to know that his cell phone and pile of bags do not make him impressive; they make him a human logjam. I want him to know that renting a stack of six porn movies a day tends to undercut his intended dashing, man-about-town effect. I want him to know that true big shots do not try to screw small locally-owned businesses out of petty amounts of cash. I want to have the pleasure of publicly deflating him.

There is no earthly reason I should care so much, and it drives me nuts that I do. I am a pacifist. I like to think of myself as a nonviolent and gentle person. I have actually fantasized about knocking Mr. Pig to the ground and kicking him. Once, when he was being particularly obnoxious, I had a flash of an image: Me putting a foot on Mr. Pig's chest, shoving a gun in his mouth, and blowing his brains across the New For Sale section. It frightened me, but I enjoyed it.

He knows my name now. He came in as I was leaving one day, just as the other clerks said "Bye, Ali!" So he leaned right into my face and said "Byyyyye, Ali!"

Now he greets me every time. I hate Mr. Pig.

Fetishists

As you might expect, we get a lot of fetishists in the video store.

If a customer is going to rent porn, I actually prefer to see a mixed bag of videos – that way all I know about him is that he wants porn. Someone comes up with a stack of five videos about people pissing for each other, and suddenly I know a very intimate thing about a relative stranger. (An interesting distinction in Illinois porn law: you can rent videos about people pissing for each other, and you can rent videos about people pissing near each other, but you may not rent videos about people pissing on each other. Go figure. There's apparently a Byzantine set of codes that have to do with taking a dump for each other, but I really don't want to know.)

Lots of people are hung up on a particular race, or a particular combination or races, and many straight men are pretty specific about breast size. (For the record, the *Nice Rack* series and the *Itty Bitty Titty* series seem to rent fairly evenly.)

The most common fetish, if you can call something so common a fetish, is for borderline jailbait. This is true of both straight and gay porn. The gay series to watch are *Eighteen Today*, *Just 18 and Gay* and *First Time Tryers*. The straight series are *Bring 'Em Young*, *Barely Legal*, and, horrifyingly, *Faces with Braces*. We actually have a guy who vets all our videos and makes sure that nobody is under 18, but still, guys who bring a stack of those up to the counter make me want to hiss and warn them away from my little sisters.

And it's never the 21-year-olds who rent *Barely Legal*, it's always the 45-and-ups. Gah. The 21-year-olds do occasionally rent the one copy of *Older Women, Hotter Sex* that we have. I approve of this, in a shocking display of my own personal prejudices.

Except for the occasional too-personal glance into their psyches, most of the fetishists don't really bug us, except for those in one special category: those who fetishize the video store itself.

They can't masturbate because of the cameras, but they do everything else. They damage the cassettes on purpose. There's at least one guy in the straight section who rips pictures off the boxes, and a guy in the gay section who apparently carries an X-acto knife.

People in both sections steal the boxes, which drives us nuts – a video without a display box won't rent because people can't see what it's about. It can take weeks to get a new, empty box and it's expensive. One guy in the gay section is definitely doing it as some kind of triumphant "fuck you" to the store – he always jams the plastic insert into the DVD rack as a calling card.

One guy called for weeks, trying to get us to special order a tape called *Autofellatio*. (By the way, I have seen the box for *Autofellatio*, and it looks like cheating to me. The guy on the cover is bracing himself up against a pool table. Dammit, if you're going to fellate yourself, do it on pure strength and flexibility or don't do it at all.) Anyway, it's a hard-to-find tape, and the guy called over and over. I talked to him twice, and I was pretty sure he was masturbating both times. When we finally found the tape, he cancelled the order, claiming he'd found it somewhere else. I think it was the act of calling that turned him on.

People do get hung up on the act of seeing or even just renting a particular video. A guy at one of our other branches rented his favorite literally hundreds of times, checking it in and then right back out. The staff begged him to just buy it, but he wouldn't. His life was destroyed when his tape was either damaged or sold to someone else. He came to our store looking for it, and wouldn't tell me the title – he wrote it down and passed the folded paper to Jeremy, the assistant manager.

Mr. Dreadlocks's particular fetish is the naughty act of renting itself. I've always had a fine relationship with Mr. Dreadlocks, but then he's gay and I don't apply to his fetish. The male clerks can't stand him, because what he likes to do is rent a tape from one of them, go home, masturbate, (we think, based on the short time he's gone, that he doesn't actually watch the tape) come back, pay for his one tape, and then pick out another and start again. Sometimes he has an erection during checkout, and once he had semen stains on the front of his pants. He freaks the shit out of the male clerks, and I understand why – it's pretty hideous to be an unwitting participant in someone else's sex act.

A lot of fetishizing has to do with unwitting or unwilling participants, and that runs pretty hard up against my "whatever floats your boat" policy. On the other hand, the more I work at the store, the more it seems like some people are just hardwired in a certain way and there may not be anything they can do about it. Which doesn't really make it OK for them to call me and masturbate or steal stuff, but what can either of us do? We're at an impasse.

But I'm still calling the cops if I catch them tearing up our boxes.

Junior Crime Dog

Part of my job is watching the security cameras downstairs. I have a love/hate relationship with the security cameras. Sometimes they're fun, but mostly it's a pressure situation. Nobody wants to have a box get stolen or ripped up on his or her shift. It's easy to keep an eye on them during slow periods, but when the register is slammed, forget it.

It's frustrating, because it's easy to tell when someone is up to no good. Thieves will come right up to the register, check a small bag, and tell you that they aren't going to steal anything. Some people give the counter a long, long look before going down, while others just try to zip past, hoping you don't see them go down at all. It's weird – people really can't seem to act normally when they're planning to be creeps. The trick, of course, is having the time to watch and catch them. Sometimes when someone's weaselling around down there, I just want to get on the Voice of God mic and say "WE CAN SEE YOU."

Winter drove me nuts because everybody dressed like a thief – bulky coats and plenty of face-covering accessories. Nowadays it's warmer (well, for Chicago) and the coat, hat, hood, scarf, and sunglasses combo stands out a little more.

Not everyone that acts suspicious is going to steal or vandalize something, of course. We spent a big chunk of Saturday watching a guy down there who was hoping to masturbate. It got sort of hilarious, in a disgusting way. He would study and study the boxes, then his hand would creeeeeeep over to his crotch… and then someone would come downstairs and wreck everything.

He had dressed well for his plan, if a little obviously – a huge coat with a big, fuzzy hood, a hat pulled down over his eyes, and baggy, low-slung pants. He kept hunching away from the one security camera he'd spotted – unfortunately giving us a great face shot on the one he hadn't.

So anyway, he'd find a box that turned him on and go over to what he thought was a discreet corner, but again, we're a little high-traffic for that, so he kept getting interrupted. Apparently in the old days it was different – no security cameras and longer dead spells. My manager used to clerk then, and she said that having to clean come out of the corners and off the walls was pretty routine.

Now there's way less masturbating privacy, which explains the upswing in box thefts. Whackers find the image they like, but have to steal it and go somewhere else if they want an uninterrupted session. And it's pretty easy to interrupt them – all the potential jerkers I've had to deal with have been huge cowards with big shame issues. Letting them know you're on to what they're up to is usually enough to get rid of them.

Finally we got tired of our visitor and decided we'd rather roust him than catch him in the act and call the cops. (Catching a customer vandalizing, stealing, or masturbating and getting him arrested means a bonus because word gets out in the dirtball network that we prosecute. So waiting to catch a guy in the act is a temptation, but then it also carries the risk that he might finish before the police arrive.) Our decision meant that I got to roust him – for some reason the other people at the store, including management, have decided I'm good at flushing people out of the porn section.

I'm not sure why, but I have two theories: The first is simply that I am pretty much the polar opposite of the women on the porn boxes. I don't know if I am a harsh dose of reality or if I remind them of their moms or their girlfriends or their wives or just the archetypical Feminine Principal or what, but straight guys hate it when I'm down there putting away tags. Sometimes simply going downstairs is enough to clear the area of dirtbags and legitimate customers alike.

I do like to think I'm pretty good at it when I actually have to card people or ask them to leave. I try to make it a face-saving situation for everyone and acknowledge that yeah, the store's 21-and-over policy really sucks. I try to be as easygoing about it as possible, especially when I have to throw out a bunch of kids.

I get sort of conflicted about throwing kids and teenagers out of the porn section. I really don't want them down there, not because I think sex is dirty or bad, but because I don't want them to think that that's what sex is about. The stuff on our boxes is sex in the basest, sometimes most brutal terms – naked women spreading their relevant orifices and making that Porn Face. Unless you're talking about the *Max Hardcore* series, which involves women with "SLUT" and "WHORE" written across their foreheads in lipstick. And besides, do we really need to raise another generation of men who can't deal with pubic hair?

So I don't feel bad about getting them out of there, except that I'm very conscious of the fact that I'm a woman while I'm doing it. I worry that I'm either setting up or reinforcing the idea that there are fun, bad women who like sex and good, boring women who restrict access to sex.

I always want to debrief them. "Hey, guys, it's cool that you're curious, but this isn't the way to find out. Porn is fine, but it's not real sex. Real sex is great, and even good girls love it, but it has to be a two-way street..." But I always just end up with "Sorry, guys. Come back when you're 21." Perhaps I should write a children's book: *Porn Is Healthy and Fine, but Only as a Temporary Physical Release.*

So anyway, I started out with the Discreet Method: I went down with a handful of tags and put away the ones right around where he was, hoping to drive him out with a quick dose of Virgin/Nun/Mom/Mother-Goddess. No dice. He just kept turning his back to me – an increasingly hard prospect as I corralled him into the corner.

He actually tried the hand creep once until he glanced over and realized I was a) an employee and b) female. He decided to wait me out, pulling his pants up and his coat down a bit. I had clearly cramped his masturbating style.

He stayed hunched in the corner and wouldn't go away on his own, so I finally broke down and asked him if he had ID and an account with us. We have a sign saying you need to set up an account to even browse down there. We don't really enforce it unless we're ousting a dirtbag, but then it comes in fairly handy. As it did in this case – just addressing him directly did the trick and he dropped his box and fled as casually as possible.

My manager high-fived me when I came up. I had kept our store clean and safe for our non-masturbating porn freaks and done my little bit to keep the virgin/whore dichotomy firmly in place.

Mom would be so proud.

Freak Magnet

Saturdays I open the store and work close to a nine-hour shift. I start out OK, but it's hard to stay cheery the whole time, even when I'm blasting Danish techno music.

I used to hate opening on weekends because the early morning customers scared the hell out of me. The store opens at 9 a.m. I usually do about 20 minutes of set-up and hit the front door at 9:00 on the dot by the store clock. There is always someone waiting to get to the porn. Once or twice I have had a problem – a register came up short or a circuit breaker was blown – and I've opened the door at, say, 9:01 and 52 seconds. In both cases, a guy was actually pounding at the door when I got to it. Not the same guy. I'm not sure whether that's scarier or not. Both guys almost flipped out when I took the time to slide the sign from "closed" to "open" before turning the lock.

It gets pretty full at 9 a.m. on Saturdays and Sundays. I don't know if people are just getting up or if they stayed up or what. I just know they've been waiting for porn until they almost can't stand it.

As I said, they used to scare me until I got to know my regulars. If you don't count the porn addiction that some of them have, they're not such bad guys. And once I thought about it, they'd be my best chance if someone tried to rob the store. They'd never let me get shot – who would give them their porn?

The not-so-regulars are still sort of scary. For some reason, I tend to draw the weirdest ones. My friends and relatives call whatever it is that seems to attract them the Crazy Magnet, but at the store they've gone with Freak Magnet.

The Freak Magnet was definitely on today – the phone started ringing before I was even open. Mr. Dreadlocks called early on, asking to reserve two movies. "OK, what are the titles?" "I can't recall." I invited Mr. Dreadlocks to call back if and when he figured it out, but he never did, and he didn't come in. He likes me, but I'm disappointing because he's hoping to get a male clerk. I'm guessing the evening shift will get that particular treat.

The most disturbing customer of the day called right at 9:00 to ask when we opened. I told him we were, and he asked if the DVD of *L.A. Sex Party* was in. (A lot of our movies have "sex party" in the title. It was only a few months ago that I realized that this is because a lot of porn renters may not know what "orgy" means.)

It was in, but today we didn't have another clerk on yet, and I can't leave the register unattended to go downstairs and all the way to the back to pull a gay adult DVD tag.

So I told him we expected one in and I could put him on the reserve list. He called back less than an hour later to see if it was in yet. He knew, as a member, that rentals aren't due back until closing the night they're due. He was clearly going to call back at half-hour intervals until I said the tape was in, which sounded like a long shift to me, so I told him the truth. I explained that I could go down and pull his tag as soon as the new clerk came in, which would be very soon. It wasn't a new release and wasn't in much demand. I told him that it was a safe bet that it would be in when he got there – especially since he said he would come right over. "Well, if someone tries to rent it, could you take it away from them?" Well, no. I explained for about the thirtieth time that another clerk would be on soon, and that it was unlikely that his DVD would rent before then. And then as politely and gently as possible I refused to rip the DVD from another renter's hands.

He got to the store before the second clerk did.

He went racing right downstairs, which wasn't that unusual – Saturday morning porn renters all but throw themselves down the stairs.

He got back up behind two other renters, who made the mistake of breaking their pace to get their tags together before hitting the register. He ran around the side and cut in front of them. The three of us not-freaks exchanged looks for a second. I almost made him wait, but then realized we all just wanted him out of there. No time for thought (or, indeed, basic courtesy) though.

"It was here!" he crowed, "I'm the one who called!" His precious DVD was in, as were two others. I took a look at him as I pulled up his account and checked his ID. He looked like he was either a hotel desk manager or a flight attendant. He had just missed pilot. He was wearing a navy blue suit with a white stripe at the wrists. He had what looked like airline wings on his chest, as well as what may have been a small brass nametag and some sort of Masonic or fraternal pin.

He caught me trying to figure it out as I checked him out. "No, I don't fly for the airlines," he said proudly.
(Because I am a good clerk, I refrained from saying "Of course not. You're dressed like a flight attendant,") "I just have a thing for uniforms," he went on, loud enough for the whole line to hear, "I'm trying to pick someone up this morning!"

And with that, he and his homemade uniform were gone.

There's a New Porn Freak in Town

We have a new visitor to the porn section. He's been in twice now. Actually, he's been in at least three times, as he is a registered member, but he's only stood out twice.

He comes in, goes down to the straight porn section, and whips out a hand mirror. Then he applies makeup for about an hour.

Seriously.

No browsing, no chatting people up, no whacking. In, mirror, makeup and out. And again, he's in the straight section.

No one's sure what to do yet.

The last time he was in, two clerks went down to ask him a) what was up and b) to leave. He pointed out that he was a registered member, and that he wasn't stealing, whacking off, or bothering anyone. Since he wasn't hurting anyone, why did he have to leave?

Nobody's thought of an answer yet, and we're not really sure we want to toss him for loitering. He is, after all, just putting on makeup.

But why in our porn section? It has such harsh fluorescent lighting.

I'm sure we'll find out eventually. I can't wait.

Guttermouth

I'm having another existential video store crisis. I have them every now and then, but this one is biggish – this Friday will be my one-year anniversary at the store. It isn't the worst job in the world. It's helped me plow through some difficult financial times, they're terrific about letting me take off for an audition, and they have twice let me take a full month off to go do a show. The pay sucks, but there's no dress code and you can't beat the flexibility.

But still, holy fuck. I know it is exactly a year this Friday because I started the job (a year ago – have I mentioned this was a year ago?) precisely one week before my thirtieth birthday. Talk about your existential crises. That one was enormous, and it came on in a single moment: I was putting away porn tags, when suddenly I looked up and came face-to-face with the box for *Fuck Pigs 5*. I can still see the box. There was, of course, a woman on it, offering up her orifices for the pleasure of anyone who wanted a look. She seemed friendly, almost shy. And she was being called a fuck pig.

"Good Lord," I thought, "What happened to me? I'm about to turn 30 and I'm on my knees in a basement restocking incredibly degrading porn."

This time around I will be about to turn 31 and I will be on my knees in a basement stocking incredibly degrading porn. At least I can laugh about it. Sometimes I have to pull my lips into a rictus grin, peel my tongue off the roof of my mouth, and punch myself in the solar plexus, but a laugh is a laugh.

I've gotten numb to a lot of it over the past year – and some of it I do find genuinely hilarious – but I am still, sometimes, conflicted about the really degrading porn. The *Fuck Pig* stuff.

It took a long time for me to even admit to myself that porn can be degrading. I'm a sex-positive, first amendment feminist. I've been through the progressive arguments about porn: lesbians enjoy it too, so porn is not inherently degrading to women; the woman giving the blow job can be very much in control of the sex act; and besides, what if in censoring other porn they decide to come for your porn first? I got them, I believed them, and I was willing to defend to my death (or at least to my jailing) the right to produce porn, assuming all the actors truly consent.

As is so often the case, I had those lofty ideals before I really had any experience with porn other than as an abstract concept. Working with porn on a regular basis, while it has expanded my whatever-floats-your-boat tolerance, has led me to conclude that yes, sometimes porn is degrading. Indeed, sometimes it's meant to be degrading. Sometimes that's the whole point.

Take, for example, the *Guttermouth* series, the latest example of which arrived last week and triggered my current case of porn clerk malaise. In a way, it was satisfyingly cyclical moment – *Guttermouth* also refers to its stars, still young enough to look happy and proud on the box, as "fuck pigs". They look about 19. They look sweet. They're posing in bikinis and looking right at the camera, hoping you will like them. Fuck pigs. The box copy is what's really revolting. It's over the top, but I don't think it's meant to be funny. There are short fake cast bios of all the girls, in the same happy tone of theater bios before the actors grow up and get hip and cynical. One of them is called a dumb slut, another a worthless cunt. I'm fairly certain there was more on the other two, but it was just too depressing to keep reading.

This is the one porn impulse that I honestly don't get. (Oh, all right. I don't really get peeing on each other or hurting each other, but I think I understand intellectually how one might get there.) I don't understand the need to degrade someone. But that need is definitely, sadly out there. One of our best-renting titles of long standing is called *Grudge Fuck*.[3] It always rents right back out as soon as we can replace the tag. Every time.

Much as I hate to say it, it seems to be a straight guy thing.

There's definitely a Captain Kirk–style exploration up and down the imaginary social ladder in both the straight and gay sections. In addition to the dozens of variations on (oddly – or sadly) still taboo interracial pairings, we have

---

[3] Actually, the title is *Grudge F*ck*. There's a picture of a guy reaming a woman right on the box. Why did they get squeamish about the F-word?

More Dirty Debutantes[4] and *White Trash Whore* on the straight side, *Straight off the Street* and *The Other Side of Aspen* on the gay side. You can fuck rich or fuck poor on either side of the invisible barrier between the straight and gay sections. But you can only fuck lesser in straight.

I think it's because there's not enough otherness in gay porn. There's still bondage and S&M stuff, plenty of dominance and submission, but even the most submissive sub is still a man just like the dom, just like the viewer. How much separation can there be?

On the straight side, it's different. One of the *Extreme Penetrations* boxes shows a woman, legs spread and sticking straight up, with some sort of funnel or bowl shoved into her vagina. It actually has pretzels in it. Rocco's *Animal Trainer* series, I'm told, traditionally ends with Rocco fucking a woman up the ass while he shoves her head into a toilet and flushes.

Some straight porn does seem to be made in sort of a happy, fun spirit: women are beautiful and fun to look at, sex is fun and good to have. Whee!

And then there's *Guttermouth*.

Is it fear? Is it anger? Is it such an unfamiliarity in dealing with women that they don't even seem like real people? Or is it, as I'm prone to suspect on difficult days, that some people are just complete shitheads? I don't know.

---

[4] I have since learned that *More Dirty Debutantes* was really about actresses who were making their debuts in adult films, not about women from the yacht club circuit getting down.

What I learned in Women's Studies is that porn is not necessarily degrading. What I've learned at the video store is that sometimes it is.

My position on porn hasn't really changed. I would still defend to my death the right to produce it. I just sometimes wish they wouldn't.

Our Heroine Has More Inner Fortitude Than She Thought.

This is – almost – a story of triumph.

I've always been worried about what I'd do if I actually caught a jerker in the porn section. I mean, of course, while I'm physically in the porn section. Catching someone on the security camera didn't bother me: Call the police and collect a bonus for busting a creep. Big deal. My only concern on that count was who's responsible for cleanup.

But actually catching someone while down there has always been a concern. I'm 5'3" – not a terribly imposing presence. While, as I've said before, most of the people who attempt to masturbate in the store are cowards, there are no guarantees. I've read more than one study that indicates that rapists start off with indecent exposure before graduating to scarier, more violent stuff. It wasn't like it was a constant fear for me, but it certainly popped into the back of my mind more than once.

And it had been in my mind recently because Jonathan caught a jerker a couple of weeks ago. By the way, it turns out the managers are willing to take care of the mopping.

The porn section is not completely isolated from the upstairs counter, but it's a hike. You could get around (or over) the counter and downstairs in maybe ten seconds. The whole section is covered by the cameras, but we usually have the sound off unless we're watching someone in particular. On the other hand, you can hear someone making loudish noises like knocking over shelves in the straight section. Essentially, one could get help from upstairs, but not without a few seconds' delay.

OK, so I have thought about it some. But I've honestly never known how I'd react. Scream? Run? Quietly go upstairs and then get help? What?

I found out this weekend. I was bored out of my skull about halfway through my usual nine-hour Saturday Shift of Doom, and I was downstairs putting tags back out. There was only one other person down there – a young guy, not a regular. I'd been keeping one eye on him anyway because he was wearing way more coat than he needed, which is the I'm-gonna-steal-a-box uniform.

We were on opposite sides of the room with our backs to each other. Gradually, I became aware of movement behind me. I turned around. His pants were drooping a few inches below the waistband of his boxers. He had snaked his right arm up underneath his coat and it was moving rhythmically.

For a second, I just stared.

Then, before I knew it, I heard a new voice coming out of my mouth. It was a furious principal's voice, a drill sergeant's voice, Sigourney Weaver's voice just as she's about to wax an alien. It came up from the diaphragm, resonating through my chest, deep, powerful and furious.

"PUT IT AWAY AND GET OUT!"

He dropped the box he'd been holding and whipped around, eyes huge with astonishment.

He had been scratching his stomach.

Interesting Porn Phenomena

1. Beth's First Law of Tag Replenishment:
Of any ten tags you need to put away, nine of them will be in front of the big creepy guy who won't move.

Ali's Corollary:
Of these nine, at least five will require you to bend or crouch in such a way that your head is right in front of his groin.

2. Porn Trance
This is the odd, timeless zone that people go into when studying the boxes. Lone porn renters go into it immediately and resent being pulled out.

Group renters never intend to go into Porn Trance. They start out laughing together, pointing at the boxes and reading particularly ludicrous copy out loud. They are far too hip to really be interes… and then they see an orifice that really strikes them and one by one they get sucked in and the porn section is quiet again.

Couples do not go into Porn Trance. There has already been a great deal of negotiating in getting both parties down there together. If either partner gets even a tiny fraction more interested in a porn star body than the other, the delicate balance – and quite possibly the relationship – is destroyed.

We have two rooms of floor-to-ceiling boxes. People in Porn Trance methodically look at every single one in their section. They don't realize they've just rented new releases because they don't realize they've moved around the entire circumference of the room. They don't hear announcements over the Voice of God mic until you get drastic. ("Sir? YOU! In the red jacket! With the baseball cap! YOU! We're closing! BRING UP YOUR MOVIES RIGHT NOW OR YOU DON'T GET TO RENT ANYTHING AT ALL!") People literally spend hours in Porn Trance. I see people look at box after box for two hours at a stretch all the time, and three hours is not uncommon. These are the same people who tell you they're in a hurry when they hit the register.

I think finding the right video is such a primal, visceral thing that people really can't think about time or comprehend verbal announcements the first time around. They've gone back down to the reptilian brain and it takes a few seconds for those higher lobes to kick back in. Or maybe, since to choose the right tape they have to sort of mentally masturbate to it, they have also mentally locked themselves in the bathroom and all other stimulus is just so much faint knocking. I don't know. I haven't asked.

3. *Porn Drift*

People who have been in the straight section for a while will, more often than you think, get progressively more adventurous. Suddenly videos featuring pre-op transsexuals (sensitively called "She-Males") start showing up. Most of the time that's all there is, but not necessarily. We do feature bisexual videos (and by that, of course, we mean bisexual men - bi-girl action is pretty much a given in the straight section) and every now and then someone you didn't expect will dip his first toe into the gay end of the pool.

There are way more bisexuals in the world than you think there are. I know there are way more than you think, because there are way more than I thought, and I'm bisexual. People who have finally gotten rid of all their inhibitions in that regard rent all over the Kinsey scale – there are a few 50/50 renters, but more people just seem to throw in what suits them. It still freaks out many of my fellow clerks when people do that. "Weird. That guy rented three gay videos and two straight," comes up a lot. I usually gently mention that there are more than two options in the world, but they tend to just give me blank looks. Oh, well – most of them are still in college. They'll learn.

I tend to notice bisexuals a lot because it's fascinating to me that there are so many more than I ever knew, but also because I really don't want them to be creeps. Some of our coolest customers rent bi, but then some of the biggest freakos do too. I'm keeping an informal mental tally and frankly it doesn't look good. I'm hoping some nice bis will step up to the plate.

But I digress. We actually hardly ever turn people gay or even bi. The clerks at our all-porn branch have noticed a fairly strict progression because their porn is broken up by far more than gay and straight. According to them, the most likely Porn Drift path for a straight male goes from all lesbian to straight sex (some guys are so freaked out about seeing another guy's penis that straight sex videos are called "gay male" in some circles) to she-male section.

We keep the transgender stuff in the straight section – straight guys do not want to go to the gay section for their chicks with dicks videos.

And for the most part, gay men don't rent them.

(I have been given two interesting explanations as to why straight guys like women with penises. The first is that men don't believe that women like or want sex as much as they do. A chick with a penis, then, is a woman who has a full, hearty, male sex drive and must want sex as much as he does. The second one is almost touching to me: Vaginas are mysterious, and penises are by comparison fairly straightforward and easy to satisfy. A guy knows what to do with a penis, so if a woman has one he can be sure he knows how to satisfy her.)

I am actually sort of heartened by Porn Drift. I like seeing concrete evidence that sexuality is a more fluid thing than people like to admit, and I like seeing people stop worrying about what they're supposed to be turned on by and just go with what they like. I feel like the more people stop trying to fit themselves into rigid little boxes, the more they'll be able to cut people slack when they fit into a different box, or don't fit into a box at all.

So depending on your point of view, we're either helping people to open up to a new understanding of themselves and others, or we're helping to turn previously normal people into depraved freakos.

What else is new?

Dirtbags

I never thought I would be the sort of person who would mentally categorize people as "dirtbags," but I am and I do. In a way, it's part of my job. Dirtbags rip up boxes, tamper with tapes, and try to steal the DVDs. They try to peel off pricing stickers and put them on movies that aren't for sale. They claim damages on tapes that are fine, they try to scam us with the punch cards, they keep movies for weeks on end and try to weasel out of the late fees. They try to masturbate.

Sometimes I don't even know what they're doing – I just know that they're dirtbags and need to be watched. It bothers me that I can spot them when they hit the door. I don't like the fact that I'm categorizing people, but then I hate getting scammed or taken more. It makes me angry, it makes me tired. So I keep an eye out for dirtbags.

There is, as you might expect, a healthy intersection between dirtbags and heavy porn renters.

I think it's partly due to the expense involved in a porn addiction – scamming is a way to cut corners – and partly that anyone renting six hardcore videos every single day of his life has already at least to an extent said his goodbyes to the laws of society. But you'd be surprised: not all porn addicts are dirtbags and not all dirtbags rent porn.

Though dirtbags do seem to have a common fondness for backyard wrestling videos and the *Faces of Death* series.

I couldn't tell you what makes a dirtbag. It's like obscenity: you know it when you see it. If I had to put it into a word, I'd go with "shiftiness". Dirtbags are trying to do something wrong and deep down in their dried-up little dirtbag souls they know it and somehow their mental can-I-get-away-with-this calculations show.

One guy actually has shifty eyes. I couldn't believe it – I'd always thought that that was one of those Victorian techniques for recognizing the Criminal Type, but damned if it isn't true. I was stunned when Mr. Creepy came up to the counter, claiming that an entire stack of porn he'd rented should be free because somehow the clerk had given him six wrong tapes, and there were his eyes, shifting shifting shifting around like beady, guilty little gnats, looking at anything in the room but me or the incriminating videos.

Mr. Creepy is the one who makes me meditate on the nature of dirtbagness the most. He is always scamming. Bogus damage reports, punch card scams, claiming he got the wrong videos, and of course moving pricing stickers around. The first three bother me the most because they take advantage of our good nature. I hate it when people chip away at our likelihood to cut a good person a break. Especially when they're just trying to save up for the next entry in the *Stop! My Ass Is on Fire!* series.

The thing is, Mr. Creepy always thinks that we're the ones trying to scam him. He sometimes will pre-pay for a movie. The flag that shows a credit to someone's account is a smallish one, and the clerk won't always see it unless the customer points it out. This is especially true in Mr. Creepy's case, since there are so many notes on his account that it lights up like a Christmas tree.

In the process of making sure he didn't tamper with the tapes he's turning in and making sure he acknowledges that the one's he's checking out are correct and he isn't stealing anything and he isn't trying to get his card double-punched and wondering why this fucker still has an account with us at all, it's easy to miss the credit. And he flips out. He thinks we're trying to cheat him, even if the clerk who did the prepayment gave him a receipt, even if we apologize.

I wonder how many times you have to get cheated or scammed or worked over by life to turn into Mr. Creepy. Did his parents teach him that or was it one event or was it a long, slow process? How do you decide that it's OK to be a dirtbag, and at what point is it OK for me to write him off as one? Yes, I know: ideally, never.

I sometimes wonder what it would take to turn him around, although I am honest enough with myself to admit that I wouldn't want to be the one to do it. Could he be turned around at this point? Or will he just spend his life committing petty scams and getting creepier? As a good liberal and a caring person who recognizes that life is a web of interconnecting influences, I feel sad for Mr. Creepy. As a clerk, I want him to get the fuck out of my life and never come back.

As I said, I am conflicted about my growing instinct for spotting dirtbags. I think I'm an equal-opportunity spotter.

I'm pretty sure that I base it on shiftiness rather than any other factors, but I worry. My friend Eric, a six-foot-something black man, was once telling me about his frequent trips to Canada. His favorite thing about Canada, he said, is that white women who see him coming down the street don't clutch their purses like they do here. Gah.

Spotting dirtbags always brings up the worry that I have prejudices that I don't know about. We did used to have a clerk that, some of us noticed, only kept an eye on our black customers. An old manager had a problem with people who didn't speak English like a native. One of our local policemen once warned me to be especially careful of my register when "fags" are in the store.

Me, I used to feel happy for elderly gay men who rent porn because they finally have an outlet after all these years, but completely creeped out by elderly straight men. Now that I've been at the store for a while, I've progressed. I'm creeped out by both.

Porn and the Differently Abled

I like to think of us a very diversity-friendly store. While many of our titles are certainly indelicate because of porn's cut-to-the-chase nature, we do feature porn starring as many different ethnicities in as many different combinations as we can find. I didn't think of this as a public service until one of our customers brought it up. He had come to our neighborhood from way, way downtown, which a lot of people do. People sometimes come in from a state away, especially gay porn renters, so crossing town didn't seem that odd to me until he commented on it: "You know how hard it is to find porn on DVD with people who look like me in it?"

So I at least had an odd pride about us providing equal access to porn... until the guy in the wheelchair came in. Our store is deliberately designed to make the porn section hard to get to. We want people to have to pass the register so the clerk can see them and we make them snake through the shelves a bit so it's hard for kids to get down there. Turns out it was a nearly impossible gauntlet for a wheelchair.

The guy was surprisingly nice about it. He'd already had a shitter of an evening. All he wanted was to rent some videos, which many of our customers do on autopilot. He had waited more than an hour for a cab to pick him up – he was on some kind of subsidy for taxi transportation, but that meant he had to wait for a specific company to bother to send a driver around. Then he had to get over our doorstep, which is wheelchair accessible in a theoretical sense at best, and weave his way through too-tight aisles only to hit a freaking staircase.

Luckily he could walk a bit. He took the railing with one hand and my arm in the other and we went down, then I went back and brought the chair down for him. With the taxi, getting him in the door, and getting him downstairs, I was now the third person who he'd had to ask for help just to rent some frigging porn. I was torn between sticking around to help – from the chair he could only reach about three shelves – and giving the poor guy some privacy. I went with moderate privacy, leaving him alone and checking out the security camera every now and then until it looked like he was done, then going down to help him back up.

...And then he had to wait over an hour yet again for another taxi, which never showed. We finally hailed him one, and a friend of mine who happened to be passing helped me help him into the not-at-all wheelchair modified cab. I think by the end of the night the total number of people who'd helpfully intruded on his porn rental was six or seven. And I think the whole trip took him about four hours. Except to return the videos, he hasn't been back and I can't blame him. A year ago, I didn't think of porn as a basic human right, but now I sort of do.

Several of our regular porn renters are mildly retarded, which brings up another prejudice I didn't know I had until I started clerking. It's amazing how little our society recognizes that the mentally challenged have adult sexual impulses, but they sure enough do.

We thought Mr. Stiff was just a pain in the ass at first. He always needs to restate everything: how many days he gets to keep his movies, what each will cost individually, what the total will be, what specials he's eligible for, and that, yes, he will in fact get them.

After a few visits, I realized that he's just covering his retardation really well. He wants to make sure he understands everything, and I think he does it in the angry, pain-in-the-ass tone of voice because it's better than being vulnerable. I think in a way he's coming from the same point of view as Mr. Creepy – he's so used to not understanding things or the rules apparently changing on him that he feels like people are trying to cheat him all the time. Mr. Creepy uses that as an excuse to scam us. Mr. Stiff just tries to make sure everything is clear.

I think he's stiff and stilted partially because he's working so hard and partly because he's nervous; he never knows when the situation is going to fall apart and turn humiliating.

I feel bad for Mr. Stiff because at some point someone apparently told him that either porn or sex itself is dirty and bad. Every now and then he'll get mad at himself, come in, cancel his account and announce that he's never coming back. He cancelled and re-opened his account so many times at one of our other branches that they told him he couldn't re-open his account any more. Now he comes to us, but he still hates that he does it.

The Symbiots used to freak us out pretty badly. It was a retarded gentleman and his nephew – or, as we feared, his "nephew". They did have IDs with the same last name, but it was a pretty common one and we were worried we had some kind of chickenhawk situation on our hands and didn't know what to do about it. The nephew was too young to go downstairs (it wasn't ridiculously creepy – he was maybe 18) but was caught down there with the uncle and rousted several times.

The problem with rousting the nephew was that the uncle couldn't pick out porn by himself. Every time they came he went though the entire gay porn section one box at a time.

He couldn't remember what he'd seen before. He couldn't remember that you bring up the tags and not the boxes. He couldn't spot the difference between the for sale stuff and the rentals. He couldn't remember that you only get to check out six movies at a time. He only wanted the cheaper old releases, but couldn't distinguish the old and new release sections.

It would take him hours, and he usually got something wrong and had to go back down. We actually debated saying screw it and letting the nephew, who was of normal intelligence, go downstairs to expedite things, but our manager nixed it.

Finally he'd get back upstairs. The nephew would help the checkout go smoothly; his job was to make the world easier for the two to negotiate.

Then we got to the uncle's half of the relationship: He had the money. He had all the money, and what's more, he knew it was the source of his power and kept a pretty tight rein on it. Occasionally the nephew would pick out a video from upstairs, but his uncle had the account, so he had to check it with him first.

The whole thing freaked all of us at the store out very, very badly.

There were a lot of worried clerkly notes on the file. We didn't know what was going on, just that it was creeping our shit. Were we supposed to do something? There was an ongoing debate as to who was taking advantage of whom.

I served the Symbiots several times and, though nobody at the store agrees with me, I came to the conclusion that it wasn't a sexual relationship. I'm even pretty sure that they really were uncle and nephew. I think they had somehow discovered that they were both gay and formed an interesting team – separately, they couldn't get porn, but together they were unstoppable.

Unfortunately, sometimes our mentally challenged customers cover so well that at first glance they come off as dirtbags. It's hard, in a quick transaction, to tell the difference between someone who is genuinely confused about the rules and someone who's trying to get around them. I usually slip a note on the file suggesting that the customer in question may need some extra assistance, but there's only so much that can do.

It can get frustrating, and I worry that I'm not doing enough. That's why I try to do my best: at least that way whatever else happens, at the end of the day I can rest secure in the knowledge that I have done all I can to make sure that every adult has an equal shot at renting *Fuck Pigs 5*.

Scandal Rocks the Video Store

You may be wondering how to scandalize a bunch of jaded porn clerks. I'll give you a hint: it's not with porn.

S. was a weird clerk to work with. For one thing, he was really into '80's hair bands. Also Nickelback, which only really became difficult after, say, the third consecutive round on the CD player. I didn't really mind that so much, though, because not only did S.'s presence drop me down to the rank of second oldest clerk at my store, it also meant that I was only the second least funky. Our store is sort of aggressively funky, but I still felt better being knocked out of the top slot.

But that wasn't the really weird thing. We all have our musical quirks, and tolerate each other's pretty well. What was weird was S.'s Superclerk persona. Like the rest of us, he wasn't at the video store bucking for a management position. He was a computer programmer, having recently graduated from DeVry ("Oh," said my mother, "Then he's really just sort of a programmer.") and was looking for a job. The store was pretty cool about keeping him working five shifts a week with the understanding that he'd drop the job with very little notice once one of his interviews paid off.

So he made no secret of being on his way out, but insisted on playing Superclerk. Actually, he was really more HallMonitorclerk. He'd automatically check the clock to see if other people were on time for their shifts – and in fact he'd comment on it if I were only on time instead of a few minutes early. Every time I relieved him he'd gleefully show me how many sales he'd made, even though we're not on commission or anything. Clerks don't really do sales except in the sense that we accept money for purchases – we don't push anything.

He'd always bitch when his shift was slow, saying he'd rather keep busy, and took careful notice of who was not as particular as he was with their cleaning assignments.

He'd complain when he found little doodles on Post-it notes around the counter – how could the night shift do these damned things when nearly every morning he came in to find the vacuuming below par? He'd get jazzed up about staff meetings for weeks ahead of time.

In short, S. was a nice guy, but an incredible pain in the ass.

A week ago Friday, I got a call at home from Matt, the guy who does all the scheduling. Would I be able to take an extra shift or two?

S. had been arrested.

In the seven months S. had been working at the video store, he had embezzled nearly six thousand dollars. And that's what they can prove – my manager thinks it may have been more like ten thousand.

The managers were all furious – they felt they had treated S. like part of the family and he had betrayed their trust. The reaction of the clerks was less visceral, but the same across the board: *Wait a minute. If he was already stealing from the store, why did he have to be such a self-righteous prick about the cleaning assignments?* It still doesn't make sense.

The bizarre thing is I don't think it was a cover. I'm pretty sure that in his own mind, S. was far and away the best clerk at the store. I don't even think he thought of what he was doing as stealing, and certainly not as grand theft. He was, after all, doing his thieving three bucks at a time.

It wasn't even a programming trick (thus adding credence to my mother's assessment). We're pretty sure he was just telling the customer the prices for their returns (which wouldn't be hard – the same combinations come up a lot) and then zeroing out the numbers in the computer as though they had free rental cards. Then he just pocketed the overage at the end of his shift.

It wouldn't be hard, and actually the anal-retentive way the store handbook suggests counting out our drawers facilitates it.

On the other hand, it was really, really stupid. It's not like we don't have accountants. It didn't take all that long to notice that S.'s drops averaged anywhere from $50–$100 less than any other clerk working the same shift, or that he gave out way more free rentals than anybody else.

I can't believe they waited as long as they did to nail him.

But nail him they did. They had him arrested and cuffed right off the register in the middle of his shift. Pretty hardcore. Apparently his parents are paying back the money he stole so he'll have a misdemeanor instead of a felony on his record. It's tough to think of many things I'd want to do less than explain to my parents that I'd been arrested for seven months of petty theft.

So S. goes free and the store gets its money back. It's the remaining clerks, of course, who will end up taking the brunt of the fallout.

The upstairs security cameras, once aimed so that we had a good view of the hands and faces of people browsing the for-sale movies, have been re-aimed. Now they give a good view of the hands of the clerks.

I was so insulted by this that I considered walking right off the job. It's ridiculous. You can see our hands, yes, but it's not like you can tell if someone is zeroing out the prices on the computer screen. The thief-magnet sale racks are now only vaguely visible in the background. Incredible.

We also got a letter in our paychecks from Bob, the owner. It describes the arrest in lascivious detail, then has a message for the rest of us about how he's sure we're all great people with big plans for the future, but he will not hesitate to bust our asses if it turns out we're not.

So there's a bit of a clampdown. Everyone's afraid to give a good customer a break on, say, accidentally bringing up the wrong tag and getting the wrong movie because we know our free rentals are being gone through with a fine-toothed comb. The cameras are always pointed at us and the general managers call about fifteen times a day to make sure everything's OK.

On Tuesday Bob stopped by at 7 a.m. – NOT to check up on me, mind you, just because he was in the neighborhood. But while he was there, how was everything going?

S. is truly amazing. He managed to be a pain in the ass one last time.

I Hope This Isn't a Trend

I caught another jerker in the porn section today. It's amazing – I'm already jaded about it. Part of it was that I just caught him on the security camera, so I had that distance, and he was really more of a stroker than a jerker. I don't think he had come in intending to masturbate. I think he just got aroused by some of the boxes. He had one hand in his sweatpants and was just sort of giving himself the occasional stroke or two as he went along.

Still, discretion doesn't make it OK to whack off in my store. I popped him up for a close-up on the monitor and, yup, that's what he was doing.

I thought about calling the police, then figured screw it. I got on the Voice of God mic and said "Sir, you need to keep both hands where I can see them."

He looked up at the camera, pulled his hand out of his pants, and continued the rest of his porn box perusal whack-free.

As he was leaving the store, I went up to him and said, "Next time you don't get a warning – I'm just calling the police." He looked at me and nodded OK. There wasn't any guilt, but there was no defiance either – he'd tried it, I'd caught him fair and square, and we both knew I'd been way nicer about it than I had to be.

To be honest, it made me feel sort of bad-ass to be so calmly and firmly in control of the store. Once I thought about it, I realized that I felt like a jolly, middle-aged madam in the Old West – ready to take care of my customers' needs in a friendly and straightforward manner, but with a strict policy against taking any guff. Shoot, they're just men. I can handle those whippersnappers.

The store is definitely changing me. I can't tell if that's a good thing or not.

Gaping Asshole Inside

Several of our straight porn boxes have a cheerful little blue circle on the front. It's designed to look like a sticker and it says "Gaping Asshole Inside!" in the same sort of cheerful font one might use for "Now with more fiber!" or "New fresh scent!"

It is clearly meant to be a feature, a sort of guarantee of quality: whatever else may or may not happen in this film, you are guaranteed at least one gaping asshole. Frequently there is also a gaping asshole holding the box, but that issue is not addressed.

It baffles me.

I understand, on an intellectual level, why porn is so focused on anal sex. It's taboo and a large segment of the female population will have no truck with it. Of course that's what guys, or at least a lot of them, fantasize about. But why even the biggest butt freak in the world would want to hunker down and take a look inside is beyond me.

But porn, or at least the porn we're carrying, is very big on taking cameras up and in and through anywhere they can go.

Part of it is a general gross-out, can-you-top-this thing that seems to be part and parcel of the adult industry – world's biggest cocks, the century's most extreme penetrations. I think porn, which doesn't have much in the way of scripting or acting chops to move it along, has to rely on other ways to convey intensity: bigger, harder, faster, freakier.

There is a new title in the straight section: *V8*. The caption says, "Four in the ass and four in the pussy!" It was the first box that has given me pause in a while.

"Sweet Jesus," I thought, "Where would everyone stand?"

Calmer reflection and the laws of physics have convinced me that they can't possibly mean penises, or at least not all at once, but I'm afraid to turn the box over and find out for sure.

I think heavy porn renters must get jaded to watching plain old sex – How could they not? – and that's what leads to the bizarre for its own sake: obesity porn, little person porn, old person porn, bondage porn, foot porn. Double penetration. Cartoonishly huge sex toys. Sticking a camera up someone's urethra. Can it possibly be sexy?

It's easy to dismiss "Gaping Asshole Inside!" as just another instance of breaking a woman down into her component parts instead of dealing with the whole being, and I almost did. I mean, ew.

But a part of me thinks it isn't just objectification. I wonder, sometimes, if the appeal of "Gaping Asshole Inside!" is one, oddly, of intimacy.

Maybe deep in his creepy little social leper soul, what the guy who picks up these boxes really craves is a woman who is so close to him that she will completely open herself to his view, someone who knows and loves him well enough to let him see absolutely everything about her. Maybe these men are looking for an act of trust as much as an act of sex.

On the other hand, maybe they're just dirtbags.

An Interesting Development

I reached an interesting new level with one of my regulars this week. He's one of my early morning guys. My favorite, in fact.

On weekdays the store opens at 7 a.m., and I've been doing that a lot lately. Mr. Gentle comes in early – not with the first rush that comes when I open the door, but before the on-the-way-to-my-9-to-5 guys. He's quiet. He always comes in not-quite-awake with his coffee and gives me a little wave before he goes downstairs.

He doesn't fuck with the boxes, he doesn't drool over the new releases, he doesn't move the tags around. He just chooses a movie or two and comes back up.

Then he turns in his old tapes (rewound, on time, and clean) and asks, "How are you?" And means it. He listens when I say "OK," is sensitive to the variation in my tone of voice when I say it on different days, and gives me a genuine answer when I ask him how he is back. He's quite literally soft-spoken, in deference to the earliness of the hour, I think, and he always says a few kind words about how godawful early I must have had to get up to be there. I like him.

It's sort of soothing to have him come by in the mornings. At least one other clerk has noticed that too – there's a note on his file that says "I wish I could option him to come in instead of some of my other customers."

Mr. Gentle is an academic of some sort. A fair chunk, if not all, of his frequent renting is due to his working on a project about representations of gender in film. It didn't occur to me until I started writing this to wonder if that's true or not, but I think it is. He's clearly both very smart and very well educated, and one day he rather fervently mentioned looking forward to the day he could stop renting all that porn. There was a note of desperation in his voice that I've only heard before from my fellow clerks.

I've asked Mr. Gentle about his project a couple of times, while we're, say, easing into the day by waiting for our ancient Etruscan credit card machine to crank up, but he's pretty vague about it. He's always said something along the lines of "You wouldn't be interested," in a friendly way. He could really mean "You wouldn't be interested," or he could mean "You wouldn't understand." I'm not sure. He's never been condescending about it in any way – as I said, he's always been friendly – but there is, as a rule, a tacit assumption among most customers that their video clerk has perhaps not been keeping up her subscription to the *New England Journal of Medicine*. (In all fairness, I haven't.)

Wednesday Mr. Gentle was in and in a fairly bad mood. Not snippy, of course, but definitely unhappy and sort of exhausted. He said he'd just been discussing his paper with someone and was upset because he thought he might have to switch the focus. He couldn't decide whether or not to risk his academic credibility a bit and write for a more popular audience.

"Worked out pretty well for Margaret Mead," I said, and looked up in time to see his head snap up and three thoughts go through his face all at once. The first was the realization that writing for a popular audience had, in fact, brought worldwide fame and respect to Margaret Mead for a solid 50 years. Hmm. Thoughts two and three were, in rapid succession, the realizations that his video clerk had not only just referenced Margaret Mead but seemed to have at least a basic handle on her career.

And suddenly we were friendlier. As I said, he's always been great, so the change was a tiny one. Now we're friendly-friendly instead of transaction-friendly.

He's always been very aware that there was a worthwhile human being behind the counter, it's just that now he's had a hint that there's a brain in the worthwhile human being behind the counter. We chatted more. I recommended an article in *Salon*, which he wrote down eagerly, and then he went away.

Today when he came in instead of hello and isn't it early we talked about the FBI scandal and what we thought the fallout would be.

I was very happy at the new nuance in our customer-clerk relationship. My intellectual vanity is, I think, the personality flaw that I've done the most work on and made the least progress with. I like him. I want him to know I'm smart and trust me to understand what his paper is about, and I like getting to talk to him a little longer in the quiet of the morning.

The downside is that now I seem to make Mr. Gentle a little sad. He seems to be fairly sensitive to nuance himself, and now I think he knows how much I don't want to be there. I want to tell him that it's OK, that things are looking up and even when they're not I'm using it all for writing fodder. But I can't tell him that because, in another nuance, while we are friendlier, we are not friends.

I'm looking forward to the day I can resign now more than ever, and in a new way. There will be a quiet pleasure in telling Mr. Gentle, when he asks, that today I am not just OK.

Wuss

First off, two updates:

1. I am pained to admit that my informal bisexual tally is not going well. The ratio is something like one incredibly cool person to every 200 complete freakballs. I am beginning to understand the origin of the unpleasant stereotyping; I'd be wary of dating me too.

2. I am deeply relieved to report that *V8* refers to fingers. How sad that I've reached a point in my life where the fact that a woman is only having four fingers jammed up her anus while another four are jammed into her vagina is a relief.

…Which brings me to M. I never actually met M. She was a new clerk we hired who quit after one day. She left a note on the manager's desk saying that she couldn't stay because the job was too degrading to women.

When I told the story to my friend Jenny, she said "Good for her!" I was taken aback for a moment, because my reaction had been "What a wuss!" Most of the women at the store had said some variation on "What a wuss!" I had told the story to Jenny in anticipation of her saying "What a wuss!"

I think the right response is somewhere in between. Some porn is degrading. Hell, a lot of it is degrading very much on purpose. It's hard to look at the box for *Young, Dumb and Full of Cum* and think the filmmakers had anything else in mind.

(On a side note, I hate it when people use the spelling "cum". I HATE IT. What, it's supposed to be dirtier that way? Just because it's supposed to be all raw and sexy doesn't mean you have to be an idiot about it. Jesus.)

But the more I've worked at the video store, the less I'm convinced that porn is inherently degrading, and the line between degrading and not gets blurrier.

For example, the [My Store] chain, (and by "chain," I mean four stores, three of which actually deal in porn) does not carry pregnancy porn. My internal reaction to that is "Good," but I couldn't tell you why. I know that pregnant women have sex. I know that some pregnant women have been frustrated by their partners' reluctance to have sex or queasiness over seeing them as sexual beings.

For that matter, it's arguably a good way for a resourceful mom to start off Junior's college fund. But we don't carry it because The Powers That Be find it inherently degrading and it's never been a point I've cared to argue. If I look at it dispassionately, though, I don't think it is. Or at least it's dependent on what the pregnant woman in question is being asked to do.

We recently stopped carrying bukkake, also because it's degrading. When I first started working at the store, that one seemed like an easy call for me. Bukakke involves a circle of men with a woman in the center. The men jerk off, covering the woman in semen. It's hard to think of a context in which that wouldn't be degrading. It certainly was hard for me.

Until, of course, I saw the box for *Gay Bukkake*. Yup. Same deal, only it's a man in the center. I realized that I found straight bukkake degrading, but gay bukkake merely incredibly disgusting. Did that make me a sexist, or was I penalizing straight men for being straight? So except for the disgusting part, I had to pencil in a new opinion.

Occasionally I get caught up in the principle of a thing, and when my manager mentioned the no-more-bukkake decision I actually started to argue with her. It took me a couple of minutes to ratchet my brain down from the logistics of it and remember that I loathe having to look at the bukkake boxes and having them out of the store would suit me fine.

So I backed out of an ethical debate and went against my newfound principles for my own comfort.

What a wuss.

The Art of the Shuffle

I've been torturing my morning customers lately.

The store has been creeping up my opening shifts over the past several months anyway, and now that S. is gone almost all of my shifts are openers. There are plenty of random freakos that shuffle in and out in the morning, but most of the people that come in at 7 a.m. are regulars.

To open the door at 7:00, I arrive at about 6:30. My rule is, if I'm hitting the door at 6:30 a.m., I can play whatever the fuck I want on the stereo to keep myself awake. Thus, the torture.

What keeps me awake is *Aquarium*, by Aqua. You may remember Aqua – they were a Danish-Norwegian technopop group that won both worldwide fame and my heart by pissing off Mattel with the song "Barbie Girl".

I honestly can't remember why I bought the entire CD. I know I wanted to use the song for something, but why didn't I just get the single? This would have been back in 97 or so when the song came out, and at the time I had a full-time job and actual disposable income, but still. Anyway, I used the song on a mix tape or something and then never really listened to the whole CD.

…Until I took this job. Shifts can become gulags of boredom without the CD player. My collection isn't exactly huge, so before long I was digging back through the pile.

And that's when I discovered that I love *Aquarium*. It's the very finest in Scandinavian synth-pop dance music. It's also incredibly chipper, in a modern Abbaesque sort of way. Years ago, I went out a couple of times with a guy who had been to Sweden and he said you really couldn't understand Abba until you'd traveled through a Scandinavian winter. I think he meant that they need that level of perkiness to keep themselves awake and sane during those endless cold nights, and I can't help but think that Aqua was doing the same public service.

Whatever they did for the Scandinavians, it really cheers me up first thing in the morning. "Barbie Girl" is great, of course, but the one that has most won my heart is the first track, "Happy Boys & Girls". After an opening synthesizer blast, the opening lyrics go like this:

Be HAPPY!
(Come on, let's go get it on!)
Be HAPPY!
Be HAPPY!
(Come on, let's go get it on!)
Be HAPPY!

And it just keeps getting better.

There's also a delightfully baffling song called "Doctor Jones":

Doctor Jones, Jones,
Calling Doctor Jones,
Doctor Jones, Doctor Jones get up now!

(Wake up, now!)
(Female lead yodels like a cowgirl)

I don't know if it's the lyrics written by non-native speakers of English or simply the relentless throbbing disco beat, but I just can't get enough of it.

Or, more accurately, I just can't open the store without it. I play it every time I open. The whole album. I can't help it – the morning just isn't complete without it. If I time it just right, I can hit "play" when I'm rounding the counter and the lead singer screams "Be HAPPY!" just as I open the door.

I am happy, but I know it's driving my customers crazy. The songs have been drilled into their brains so many times that some of them unconsciously sing or whistle along. But not in a good way. There tends to be a bit of eye-rolling when they hit the door. Straight guys hate it the most, of course. It's hard to shop for rugged, manly porn to high-pitched singing and bouncy synthesizers. I hope that both "Barbie Girl" and the underrated "For Once in Your Life, Be a Man" give them something to think about, but I doubt it.

I feel bad for them, but I can't stop. (Well, I mostly feel bad for them. A tiny, sadistic part of my brain that I can't quite get rid of sees their pain and laughs like Renfield at their torment. The only one I've actually apologized to is Mr. Gentle. He sheepishly admitted to enjoying it, solidifying his position as my favorite customer ever.)

When I first started at the store, we weren't allowed to play whole albums. Our old manager hated being subjected to one choice for an hour at a time, so he mandated filling the player with different stuff and shuffling.

I hated it at first, but then I really got into it. The challenge of creating really good shuffle is endlessly entertaining, and appreciated by all clerks, no matter what our musical tastes. For a while Casey and I were really into Bollywood soundtracks, and, really, anything that would make the customers look up at the speakers in an attempt to figure out what the hell we were playing. Casey eventually got his hands on some Tuvan throat-singing, which was a delight.

Roy Orbison, the *Trainspotting* soundtrack, Soul Coughing, and any good new wave collection used to be a favorite blend of mine, though Casey came up with the most elegantly simple mix: Belle & Sebastian and GWAR.

Constructing theme days were fun, but after a while we just got into trying to crack each other up. Someone found a Stryper CD in a bargain bin somewhere and it was in the player for about three solid weeks.

But, as I said, I pull fewer and fewer night shifts and there's a high turnover – now that mini culture is gone and we're back to throwing stuff in to suit ourselves.

If my CDs send a message, it is, generally, "Be HAPPY!" That's because I'm sort of over it. Most CDs that we play

– and I am occasionally still guilty of this – send this message: "We are cooler than you."

The clerk is of course automatically cooler than the customer because we are accepted by the public at large as snotty arbiters of movie taste, and also because anybody with a shit job is automatically cooler than someone with a 9-to-5. Too bad, no arguing, we're cooler. Our store is a nasal jewelry, snotty film school sort of place and we employ people coldblooded enough to work with hardcore pornography every single day of our lives (Oh, all right. Just every shift.), so there are plenty of extra bonus cool points right there.

I have actually had word come back to me that people sometimes hate coming to our store because they feel their relative coolness is being rather harshly judged. I, as the least cool clerk (Cf: S.'s firing), sometimes feel bad about this, but many of my fellow clerks don't.

Music underlines that point, especially if it's scary music. Some of the clerks really like death metal – the kind of stuff that goes so far over the top that I end up pissing them off by giggling at it. I don't like death metal, but it does perform a valuable function – it puts a big, scary wall of cool between us and our customers. And nothing clears the porn section out faster after a long evening. Mason used to turn it up so loudly and so suddenly that we'd all run to the security monitor to see people flinch.

It sound childish, and it is, but sometimes it's there for a reason. We have a lot of whacked-out people coming into the store. Sometimes it feels like it helps to have a soundtrack of tough playing. It makes me feel like a puffer fish: "Back off, damn it," says our music, "There might be poison in here!"

But as I said, I'm over it, and the mornings are a little lower-key. I don't care if people think I'm cool or not. I just want us all to be happy.

This week I made an important sale-bin discovery: *Aquarius*. Another Aqua CD. I'm really going to enjoy it if I can hear it over the sound of Renfield laughing.

World's Largest Cocks

I sometimes worry that the porn section may be destroying my sense of proportion. I spend at least part of every shift face-to-face, as it were, with almost cartoonishly huge cocks.

The women's bodies on porn boxes are out of proportion too, but not to the extent that you'd think. I see a lot of fake breasts, sometimes distended to the point that they must be uncomfortable. I'm not just talking about the unwieldy size; on a few women the flesh of their breasts is stretched so tightly that their nipples are distorted. But that's rare – usually it's just the standard eerily spherical balloon breasts. Don't men know that real breasts hang? (Actually, I don't really believe that men can't spot fake breasts. I think they're just happy to have any breasts around and don't care whether they're real or not. In a bizarre way, it's sort of a friendly policy.)

The implants, while definitely a major part of the straight porn world, are less omnipresent than you'd think, though. Many boxes, most notably those in the *Real Naturals* series, now promise that they only feature real breasts. And the porn industry, in its eagerness to please, has realized that many men don't even want big breasts. The young-stuff movies in particular, like the *Barely Legal* series, feature smaller-proportioned women. I guess it's easier to pretend that a girl is jailbait if it looks like she could still have some breast development to go.

Eugh.

But anyway, I'm not really worried about losing my sense of proportion for female bodies. For one thing, I've got one of my own for reference, and for another I see normal female breasts every day. So do you. Even when they're clothed, they're pretty much out there. There are plenty of ordinary, walking-around reference points to keep a person in scale. (Now that I think about it, I'd be interested to know what body issues come up in, say, Inuit society.)

But with penises, I worry. Unlike breasts, you really don't see them until (one hopes) you get fairly friendly with their owners. There's just as not as much basis for comparison.

And as badly distorted as the female porn body can get, it's nothing compared to what happens to the men.

There's a series in the straight section called *Mr. Eighteen Inches*. Eighteen! Apparently twelve isn't even impressive anymore. The gay section has the *Cocks as Big as This Box* series. I find this title hilarious, because while I know they're only talking about length, I always picture all three dimensions. Where would they find pants?

Both the gay and straight sections have giant cock fixations. The straight section tends to be more graphic about it, usually showing just pictures of women posing with a giant cock and no guy attached at all, like they didn't have room for him in the picture. The gay section – though it certainly has some crude and graphic exceptions – tends to be a little more demure about it. The men are clothed on the front, then naked on the back. Usually the guy on the front just has his penis outlined through his clothing. Wet clothing is very popular. I think it's a nice way of handling it. The customer gets the idea that the cock in question is giant, erect, and undoubtedly throbbing, but it still leaves a little mystery.

(The exception is in the videos for guys that love foreskin. Uncut movies usually feature naked, flaccid cocks on the front.)

Anyway, stuff in the gay section definitely shows a healthy interest in larger-than-average plumbing, but there's also just as big an interest in beautiful men in general. For every box with a giant penis on the front, there are two more that just show a smiling, handsome man from the waist up. Clearly said handsome man has spent mind-numbing amounts of time at the gym, but at least he's not asking you to inspect his genitals.

(By the way, the guys on the gay boxes aren't just handsomer. They also seem nicer, somehow. The guys on the straight boxes are always frowning or grimacing or just looking mean. I understand that you don't need [or want] a handsome guy in a straight film, because holy shit, what if the straight guy watching it gets a little bit attracted? But I haven't figured out why the guys on the straight boxes can't look friendly.)

Here's what the straight boxes have taught me, though: guys are the ones who care about giant cocks.

Not women, guys.

Especially the straight ones.

I understand porn's fascination with giant members because it's a visual medium and, let's face it, a dumb one. Giant cock is the quickest shorthand for virility. Big muscles = big strength, so why shouldn't big penis = tremendous power to satisfy?

Men are the ones who think a dick needs to be big to be satisfying. Sure, there are a few size queens out there, but as a rule women are way less picky about size as long as the owner of said penis learns to use it correctly.

That's actually the heart of the problem – men assume that more penis automatically means more satisfaction, when in fact it has very little to do with it. I've known more than one woman who's been initially delighted to discover that she's with a larger man, only to realize to her disappointment that he thinks that all he has to do is be large. Conversely, one hears that overcompensation can be a lovely thing.

While I'm on the topic, I'll mention another quick gender-based misconception: when men refer to big, satisfying cocks, they talk in terms of length. Case in point, *Mr. Eighteen Inches*. Women, to the extent that they care at all, care about girth. When was the last time you heard a woman say "Wow, I bet that guy could really bruise my cervix!"?

But again, when it comes to the porn section we're not talking about anything in the normal human realm here. It doesn't even look like fun.

The porn box women, of course, love these huge genitals. There's even a series called *Chasing the Big Ones*. I think it's another form of metaphor – women who want giant cocks must really, really like sex, right? Insatiable means insatiable. Or something.

I think the reason straight guys like enormous schlongs, apart from the whole bigger = more powerful and more potent thing, is that it's an easy answer to Freud's unanswerable question: what do women want?

The real answer is too hard. Women want you to be independent but emotionally available. They want you to be attached but not smothering. They want time and attention, and also some time alone. They want you to grow and change with them. They want you to be all kinds of things, and it's going to be a different list for every woman, and that list is always subject to change without notice.

For some men, and many of my regular porn addicts, I think, fall into this category, the answer is that women want you to change that glaring personality flaw and learn to talk to them like a human being. Maybe they want you to take a frigging shower.

The other way is so much easier: What do women want? Enormous, glistening cocks. If you've got one, great, your job is done. No need to worry about anything else. If you don't, well, then if women don't like you it's not your fault.

But then, none of that applies to the gay section and I'm not a guy so who am I to speculate?

I guess guys like big cocks because they're so frequently told that that's what manhood is all about. Sure, he donated a kidney to his daughter and all, but I hear he's hung like a gnat.

I feel bad for guys. There's definitely a lot of male pressure involved, but women are guilty of their share of tiny penis jokes. It's awful to feel like your body is inadequate – I wish we as a gender wouldn't participate in perpetuating that particular bit of hurt.

There's a "clinic" that drops fliers in our store every few days. They say "BIG ENOUGH?" and of course they're for penile enhancement surgery. What I've heard about breast enlargement surgery is that it's painful and dangerous, that the implants can leak or harden and cause all kinds of physical problems. I can't imagine that penile surgery is any safer or less painful, and all for what sounds like less than an inch of "improvement".

The fliers, when I see a new batch, become my good deed for the day. I throw them out.

Can't Stop the Music

I'm a monster.

Since my purchase of the second Aqua CD I've become positively Satanic about my musical choices. I do genuinely love it, but I also have to admit it's feeding a mean streak I never knew I had.

It started with just a nearly two-hour Aqua block at the beginning of my shift. Then I dug out the Right Said Fred CD. Right Said Fred are those British weightlifter/musicians who did "I'm Too Sexy," though if you ask me, the best cut on the album is the magically bouncy "Don't Talk Just Kiss."

That was an excellent three-hour set (OK, yes, that's cruel and unusual. But damn it, if you're looking at porn for three CDs worth of time you've got to be prepared to take the consequences.), but recently I've started mixing it up. I'll play two of the three, then slip in a CD of something other people actually like and then go back to the dance music. I stun them with two quick jabs and then make them wait for the haymaker.

Again, my primary purpose is not to torture my customers. It just happens to work out really well that way. (Actually, they don't all hate it. Every now and then I'll catch someone dancing on the security monitor, which pleases me to no end. One guy who was all alone started doing the Bus Stop.)

I'm still closeted about it with the other clerks. I tend to time the more socially acceptable music for when my relief comes in. I don't know what I'll do when they discover me. Run into the swamps, I guess, and spend the rest of my life in hiding, quietly humming "We Are the Cartoon Heroes".

I don't know when it will end. I can pull an opener without caffeine, but not without Aqua.

Women Who Aren't on the Boxes

Today was a banner day, of sorts. Four women went into the porn section. They went down in pairs, a couple of hours apart.

Two were straight girls out for an afternoon who went down to browse. They had shopping bags with them, and seemed like they pretty much just wanted to see what it looked like. They just sort of wandered around a bit, keeping their distance from the shelves except for the occasional swoop in to look, and then left without getting anything. (The store is a bit notorious in the neighborhood and people do sometimes just wander in to see that, yup, there's porn, and then leave.)

The other two were a lesbian couple. They were there with more purpose. One came up to the counter and asked if we had lesbian porn, then they both went downstairs to look. They scoped the place out pretty thoroughly, made a couple of selections, then came up and set up a membership. I was glad they found something they liked. While we do have lesbian porn, we don't really have porn that's aimed at lesbians. I'm not sure how to back up that statement. Arguably, hot chicks having sex with each other is aimed at much at lesbians as at straight men... only it isn't. It's just the feel of the thing - a general "Hey, fellas! Getta load of this!" vibe.

Maybe I'm imagining it, but I don't think so. We don't get much repeat lesbian business. In fact, there's only one I've seen who has ever come back, and her visits are months apart. I just don't think there's much here for her.

Anyway, I was surprised at the sudden surge of female traffic. I can go for weeks on end without seeing a woman down there at all.

I know there is porn aimed at women in the world, but we don't really carry it. I try my best to help steer the women who do come in towards something they'll like, which is difficult. For one thing, porn is a pretty personal choice, and for another, I don't actually know that much about it. The last thing I want to do at the end of my shift is check out a little porn. (This is true of the guys too, actually, and sometimes it freaks them out. To be a 20-year-old male and numbed out to porn is, apparently, a scary thing.)

In the interest of good clerking, I did finally ask my manager and learned to steer my straight female customers towards Wicked Video stuff, which have budgets and stories and nobody gets called a dumb cunt on the box copy.

I think I'm a pretty good guide. The women who do come in solo – and they are very, very rare – are usually pretty uncomfortable about it.

It doesn't help that our porn section is a completely white room with a white linoleum floor lit by bright white fluorescent lights broken up by security cameras and wall-to-wall orifices. It hits somewhere between futuristic alien clinic and porn carnival.

If our decor makes a statement, it's "Hey, fucko! Don't masturbate!" It's just not a cozy or welcoming place. So I try to be both as businesslike and as gentle as possible. I want them to know that it's fine and normal to rent porn, and that they're safe. Sometimes I'll ask another clerk or a manager to cover my register and go down with them. It seems to help get them acclimated.

Usually the women who come in are half of a straight couple. They cover the full range of comfort and discomfort. My favorite was a pretty girl with a peaches-and-cream complexion and a Laura Ashley flowered dress. When I went down to ask if she and her boyfriend needed help, she belted out "Yes! We want to BUY!" while he stood blushing in the corner.

Most are pretty quiet, though, and usually let the guy take the lead.

I don't think it's that women are less sexual than men. I think they could or would like porn if the situation were different. There are still fairly big taboos about women admitting to being interested in porn – even for the ones who rent pretty racy stuff from upstairs. And the movies would have to be different, I think. There'd have to be more about why these people are having sex. A better reason than Tab A fitting into Slot B, at least.

And, from what I do know about porn, the sex would have to be different. It doesn't look like the women on porn boxes are having that much fun. They're always being bent or twisted into uncomfortable positions, or trying to avoid sperm being shot directly into their eyes. The fact that the men watching want to see as much as possible means that the women don't seem to be getting touched much. They're just getting poled by some guy who's apparently deliberately avoiding their erogenous zones. Whee.

So we don't get many women downstairs.

I hope the few brave feminine souls who do go down there find what they're looking for.

Oh, by the way...

Management found out about this journal and the NPR piece over the weekend.

I am not fired.

Men and Women and Porn

Here's what I've learned in my year-and-change as a porn clerk: men like porn.

Admittedly, my sample is skewed because many men come to our store just for the porn and have other accounts elsewhere, but almost all of the men who come in do eventually go down to the porn section. And I don't mean "almost all" in the 90% sense, I mean all but maybe two since I've started working there.

This is a lesson because I now understand that pretty much any man I date is going to at least occasionally enjoy pornography. I don't think a lot of women have fully dealt with that. If one reads the advice columns, a lot of women can't even deal with the idea that their mate masturbates at all. Ladies, please. Chill out.

What the porn section has taught me that I think many women don't understand is that porn is a physical thing for guys, not an emotional one. It seems to be a quick, physical release. It's a way of feeling good and making sure the plumbing is still in working order and that's about it. With the exception of the addicts, I don't think it has any more significance than grabbing a burger when you're hungry or standing up and stretching when you've been trapped in a car all day.

Many women are jealous of or threatened by porn, and we shouldn't be. The key is the difference between your dog, which is a Sheltie-terrier mix that hides under the bed during thunderstorms, has a passion for cat food and prefers tug-of-war to fetch, and the general dogness of the "dog" in the dictionary.

I think a woman in a porn movie, as a rule, is taken as a general woman rather than a specific woman. She is there to stand in for general womanness. (And, based the number of rewind fees I dish out, once the viewer comes she ceases to exist.)

I think guys rent porn as a way to have the pleasure of sex without the added complexity of having to tend to someone else's needs. Which doesn't mean that he's a bad guy or won't do plenty of tending later, it's just that right now he just wants to wolf down a burger.

In a way, a guy who is renting a porn video is courteously having his selfish sex on his own time so he won't bother you with it. And "selfish" isn't a bad thing here. It's also selfish to take a hot bath and read a book by yourself, but it's important to do that every now and then.

And besides, if you had a choice between your guy renting a video and renting a person, which would you choose?

Now that I've cleared up that little misunderstanding for all time, here's what men don't understand about porn: Women do take it personally. When a woman sees your porn rental, she is likely to conclude that that is what you want. The sex act in question, the level of communication, the inflated porn body – all of it. In all likelihood, she doesn't see the woman on the box as a convenient avatar of general womanness, she sees her as tangible proof that what the owner of said box really, truly wants is a nineteen-year-old emaciated blonde with enormous fake breasts and a deep desire to take it up the ass.

This is why a gentleman is very, very careful about leaving his porn lying around the house.

Communication can also help and all that, but, hell, I'm not an advice columnist. I just think, based on what I've seen, that men and women look at porn very differently and it can't hurt for both sides to take that into account.

I think it's cool when couples rent porn together, and I'm impressed with how much they had to do to get there, or with what I hope they did, anyway.

I know it's fashionable again to say that men and women are fundamentally different – God, I cannot wait for that particular social pendulum to swing back – but I don't think they are, or at least not in this case. I think attitudes toward porn have a lot to do with socialization. There's a pressure to overpersonalize sex on one side, and to depersonalize it on the other. As always, I think moderation is a good way to go.

Figuring this out has helped me understand my customers better, I think. Knowing the guy is watching for general sex and not specific sex makes it easier to see why we have those four-hour clip jobs of just come shots. Keeping in mind that what our clients are renting is physical and not emotional or mental keeps me from caring too much about what they're renting, and in many ways that detachment is a key part of my job. (Trust me: the guy with the Iowa driver's license and the wedding ring does *not* want me to care about the fact that he's renting gay porn.)

In a way, I keep learning the same lesson over and over again: just because people's tastes don't match mine doesn't mean they're wrong. Soon, I hope, it'll stick.

Do Not Feed the Clerks

I've never understood why people give us food, but they do. I mean, yeah, none of us are working there because we're so bored with collecting those interest checks on our trust funds, but there are plenty of starving brethren in the customer service industry. Why us?

The first couple of times a customer offered me food, I kept saying "No, thanks" as politely as I could. One guy kept pressing an "extra" doughnut he'd bought on me so eagerly that there was no way in hell I was going to eat it. I was new then and the possibility of someone replacing the Boston Creme with roofies seemed like a very real possibility, so I finally just took it and threw it away as soon as he was out the door. I couldn't figure out the impulse. While I've been fond of many a video clerk in my past, it never occurred to me to feed them.

Like everything else, though, I've gotten used to it. People have given us stuff on Christmas, Easter, and the Fourth of July. One guy has, on more than one occasion, brought us cookies. Really good ones from a gourmet store. He's neither one of the creepiest customers nor one of the chattiest. He'll perk up if we say hi, but it's not like he's hanging around dying to be our friend. Why the baked goods?

I finally adopted a policy of eating food that customers had dropped by, but only if one of the other clerks has eaten it without incident first. Perhaps it was wrong to use my coworkers as mineshaft canaries, but trust me, they'd have eaten it anyway.

Our main benefactor, though, is Mr. Tint. Mr. Tint was the first regular I got to know, and that was at the angry insistence at the other clerks. I was working a night shift and the phone rang.

"Who's your daddy?" said the voice on the other end. It was my first week and I'd already fielded several prank calls, so I hung up.

He called back: "Who's your daddy?" I hung up again. I mentioned to the other clerks on duty that I'd just fielded two prank calls from the same idiot and when I told them what he'd said they almost strangled me with the phone cord. Apparently that was Mr. Tint's way of saying hello. Once you correctly identified him as your daddy, he'd bring by food.

Lots of food. Enough for everybody to eat dinner and then some.

Mr. Tint works in several capacities in the food industry and has access to a lot of it. He brings it by all the time – usually a couple of times a week at least.

I wouldn't eat it for a long time; it was just too weird. Casey, who started just a little before I did, was creeped out by it too. His theory was that Mr. Tint was fattening us up to eat us, and he was only mostly kidding.

Eventually, though, we all succumbed. We've all had more than one evening in which we weren't sure how we'd get dinner if Mr. Tint didn't drop by.

What he got out of it, of course, was a shitload of free rentals. Management knew what was going on and winked at it, figuring that it was a pretty good perk for the clerks at very little cost to the store. Like several tipping situations I've been in, the value of what he was bringing by was way, way more than he'd have spent if he'd simply paid for his videos. (On the other hand, I don't know that he paid for it. I ran into him at a mailing store once and he had some sort of goods-for-services thing going on over there too. I think Mr. Tint enjoys living by the barter system and feeling like he's getting away with something.)

But he also got a very special regular status at the store, the kind Mr. Buddy would kill for. Mr. Tint, having delivered his manna from heaven, would choose his videos (or pick up the ones we'd held behind the counter for him) and then hang out and chat. We're talking 45 minutes at a time of chatting, customers or not.

It was a delicate situation. He definitely made it difficult to properly attend to our other customers, and there was at least one incident before my tenure in which Mr. Tint so distracted the clerks (and blocked their view of the sales racks) that several items were stolen while he chatted away.

It's difficult, though, to ask someone to piss off when your mouth is full of his pizza.

Mr. Tint is still a regular, but his glory days are over. S's firing made head management go through the free rentals with a fine-toothed comb, and our side of the barter is no longer available. Our assistant manager told him as gently as possible that he'd have to pay for his movies, but it was still a hard transition.

He still chats a lot, and still lays a tacit claim to super-regular status, which we have to explain to the newer clerks. Sometimes he'll even drop by food, but without the free rentals the joy is gone.

I'm sort of glad it's over. He saved my bacon on many an evening, but it was weird to take his food, even when he was getting something out of it. He could barter free rentals, but not quite the friendships he seemed to be hoping to get out of it, and that was awkward, to say the least.

People still drop by food sometimes, but I've returned to my old policy of not eating it. I don't really think people want to poison us, but until I feel like I have a better handle on what they do want I don't feel right accepting it.

Home Is the Sailor

I've been back at the store for just over a week after all my summer traveling. I was away for a wholesome vacation to national parklands with my family, then off to an actual performing gig with my improv group. The family trip included my (much younger) little sisters and the show was in a foreign country where porn is illegal (though I hear they're having a bit of trouble with the Internet) so my vacation was blissfully, totally porn-free. I'd sort of forgotten that that's how my life used to be – no involvement whatsoever with the secret desires of total strangers.

I wish the transition back had been a harder one, but no. I slipped right back into my World of Orifices without batting an eye.

My first day back I actually picked up a shift at one of our other locations; after all that gallivanting around, I need the hours. It doesn't have nearly as good a spot for foot traffic as my branch, so the day got pretty boring. I knew that a lot of our regulars have memberships at both stores, and I could't stop myself from checking:

They hate Mr. Pig too.

Since then I've been back at my usual branch, trying to get back up to speed. I'm off my game a bit – I used to get compliments on how well I rattled off the New Membership Speech, but now I have to stop and think about it.

New Memberships, by the way, suck. They suck hard. I know they keep the store in business and all, but good lord, do we hate them. They take a clerk out of commission for anywhere from 5–10 minutes (which is not so much during the midmorning lull, but an eternity during the 4 o' clock rush) and if two new memberships get going at once, forget it: we've created a traffic snarl that's not going to get untied for the next hour or so.

No one ever listens to the New Membership Speech. By the time we get through all the paperwork and the ID checks they just want to get the hell away from the counter and rent some frigging movies and they don't want to hear it. We could tell them they have to give us hair and urine samples with every return and they'd just nod and step up their get-on-with-it body language.

We are, in fact, telling them important information like the fact that we don't have an after-hours drop box, but it's a lot to take in all at once and people just glaze over. Which doesn't help either of us a week later when they're back at the counter, this time seething with rage over late fees.

I'd be more sympathetic if there weren't a big sign over my head outlining the very same policies covered in the New Member Speech. People almost never read the sign – not even a glance at it to see what sort of information it might contain if they chose to read it at some later date.

The quickest way for a new member to win instant and massive goodwill from me is to actually read the sign. "Now how much are rentals – oh, it's right up there!" is sweet, sweet music to my ears. This is a customer who makes an effort to adjust to new surroundings by looking for and absorbing helpful information. This is a customer who will return his late films and accept his fees with grace, knowing that said late fees were his own fault. This is a customer who will not bitch about the fact that he didn't return his movies on Labor Day because he assumed that we'd be closed and how the hell was he supposed to know we'd be open? because he saw – and read – the giant sign to that effect that was posted on the front door.

But most people don't read the signs and they zone out during the speech and they get really angry about late fees. They feel violated. Even though they had both written and verbal warnings of our policies, and even though we gave them a printout with the due dates on it. I know that late fees suck, but fewer than half of our customers seem to be able to psychologically deal with the fact that they're the ones who checked out the movies and they're the ones who kept them late.

My favorite angry-customer tactic is stalking off and threatening to go to Blockbuster. They think they are cutting us to the core and that we'll run to them and hug their knees and beg for forgiveness. Well, no. The local Blockbuster has a truly crappy selection. Godspeed and welcome to it.

But I digress. Other than a higher-than-usual Crazy Magnet setting, my first week back was uneventful. I've mostly been trying to get up to speed with what the new high-demand porn tapes are and doing a bit of quiet mourning over the dismal performance of my Employee Picks shelf. You people don't know what you're missing.

Ali's List of Employee Picks that Nobody Ever Rents
American Movie
Heavenly Creatures
The Haunting (original, thank you very much)
The Interview
The Manchurian Candidate
One False Move
Run Lola Run
Say Anything
Shadow of a Doubt
Strictly Ballroom
The Warriors

I Don't Date My Customers

That's not a set personal policy, really, just the way it's worked out. I don't date my customers and I don't imagine that I ever will. (Mr. Gentle, for the record, rents gay, and for this and a few other reasons I've always worked under the assumption that he's not a romantic prospect. So those of you who have written me about him can chill out. But thanks.)

I'm not saying it's never crossed my mind. When I first thought about video clerking as a temporary supplemental career, everyone I knew seemed to have a story about a crush on a video clerk. "Oh, my God!" My sister swooned, then launched into a tale of the young god who used to work at her local store. She was not alone, and I had high hopes.

I'd never had a crush on a video clerk, but there had been a quite a few I'd really wanted to impress. I think the allure has something to do with the combination of intimacy and aloofness, and, whether warranted or not, the previously mentioned sheen of Video Clerk Cool.

I've certainly developed crushes on a few rental histories. Mr. Scruffy's is almost too good to be true – it's almost a film education in itself. All the classics, all the indies, all the greats. It's intimidatingly good, really – the kind of rental history that both inspires me to expand my film knowledge and makes me feel like a complete troglodyte for having rented and enjoyed *Deep Blue Sea*.

While Mr. Scruffy has the rental history I wish I had, Ms. Leather Jacket has pretty much the rental history I do have. Sure, lots of capital-G Good stuff, but also a healthy appreciation for *The Evil Dead II*.

But something always gets in the way. For one thing, I'm very much aware that it's creepy for me to be noticing what people rent at all, so I do make a sincere effort to cut it out. And a great rental history doesn't necessarily mean I'd actually enjoy watching movies with its creator. There are plenty of scumballs with excellent taste in movies.

(By the way, while I'm on the topic, having good taste in movies does not absolve you of all video crimes. If you're one of the dirtsacks who keep stealing our rental copies of *Wet Hot American Summer* and *The Big Lebowski*, please be aware that this does not make you a resourceful collector, it makes you a fucking thief.

Yes, even if you are white and middle class and in college. Even if it's all to feed your sophisticated appreciation of Japanese animation. You are a fucking thief, and you're no better than the guy downstairs who reeks of stale whiskey and is trying to tear pictures off the porn boxes with his teeth. Please keep that image in mind the next time you sit down to watch your ill-gotten copy of *Akira*.)

But I digress. The main barrier to dating my customers is the fact that virtually all of my male customers (we don't get many lesbians) end up down in the porn section. I'm aware – very aware, nowadays – that any man I date will probably rent and enjoy porn while I'm with him, and that's fine. But that doesn't mean it's something I'd like to chat about right off the bat. I've had a (very) few customers try to flirt or hit on me, but it's just too weird. I think they've forgotten that they're in the middle of renting porn, but I haven't. Essentially, they they're being their very most suave with me and then ending by saying "See you later – off to masturbate!" It's just too much to know.

I used to have pretty good conversations with one of my customers a few months ago. He was a nice guy, and we had similar-though-not-identical tastes in movies. We had some pretty good debates, chewing over things like why I ended up hating *Fire Walk with Me* and why he ended up loving it. He started sort of flirting and I started thinking about it. Thinking favorably, in fact.

He's African-American and I'm white, which suddenly became relevant on the day that he came in, browsed and chatted a bit, flirted a bit, then went downstairs and came up with five porn titles, all from *Black Dicks in White Chicks* and other similarly-themed series.

I told this story to a few friends, all of whom had the same reaction: "Did he realize what he was doing?"

I don't know if he knew what he was doing or not when he brought the tapes up, but the minute I glanced at the tapes we both knew it was the wrong thing. It was just too weird. We'd destroyed the impersonality of his porn rental by chatting, and made the chatting way too personal with his porn rental.

It's the polite fiction again. Sure, flirtation or an invitation on a date implies at least some sexual interest, but there's something to be said for a little mystery.

He didn't come back to the store for a long time, which I think was more comfortable for both of us, and now we don't chat anymore, which is too bad.

So as I said, I don't think dating my customers is ever going to happen, largely because I get to know them in reverse – I learn about their deepest kinks first, and then I get around to learning their names a few months later. It's just as well. When it comes to the porn section, it's more comfortable for everyone if I stay disengaged.

Mr. Hazy

Mr. Hazy was one of the first customers I got to know at the store – certainly the first name I learned. Like anywhere else, the first people I learned at the video store were the complete nightmares and the really nice ones (we have lots of normal customers; I just don't need to write about them) but Mr. Hazy was an exception to that rule. I learned him first simply because he was at the video store all the frigging time. Like Mr. Buddy, he spends literally thousands of dollars a year in porn rentals.

He's like clockwork: In, six hardcore porn videos, and then back again within a day or at most two. He does have to stagger his schedule a bit – Wednesdays and Fridays are New Porn Days and he can't miss those, so it's tough to fall into a strict two-day rhythm what with these darn seven day weeks we insist on keeping.

Besides, sometimes he gets through six videos in a day just fine.

That six videos in a day thing used to astonish me – it seemed superhuman – but then I got clued into the fact that many of the heavy renters are doing a lot of fast-forwarding. They have to burn a lot of video to get to what they want.

At least I hope to God that's what they're doing. How could you spend twelve hours a day, every day, masturbating? Wouldn't you get bored? Would calluses eventually become a problem? Some of our six-a-day customers, obviously, are just pirating our tapes, but not all of them. I know. Trust me.

I don't know why five or six videos a day creep me out but not, say, three. Why should six solid hours a day of masturbation be a reasonable amount of time? I have no idea. It's something internal that I can't seem to logic away: I have no problem with three or four hardcore pornographic videos a day, but five or six is excessive. Perhaps I shouldn't have children.

Anyway, Mr. Hazy is definitely not pirating. As I mentioned, Wednesday and Friday are New Porn Days and he has to hit them because he has seen all of our other straight videos.

I'll type that again: He has seen all of our straight videos. Try though we do to rotate the stock, we just can't keep up.

That, my friends, is why I feel comfortable using the phrase "porn addiction".

Mr. Hazy isn't the only one who has finished off the store. There are several customers that have seen everything we carry, or at least everything that floats their particular boats. That's why I loathe New Porn Days. We don't get the new stock out on the shelves until 4 or 5 p.m. at the earliest – sometimes we don't even receive the shipment until then – but people start calling at about 10 in the morning and the frequency of the calls and intensity of the whining only increase as the day goes on. (Mr. Hazy, to his credit, knows the system and doesn't show up until 4:00.)

People want to paw through the new boxes. The want us to bring them over to the counter so they can stare at them. They want us to read off the new titles, never mind the woman with three small children standing at the counter. They want to see and touch and rent the new tapes, and they want them *now*.

I haven't quite pegged exactly why people get so frantic over New Porn Day, or why it's so important to be the first person to rent the new movies. I think part of it is that, yeah, they've seen everything and here's a new shipment of new bodies and new fucking and another shot at or variation of whatever they're looking for, but I also think it has something to do with the firstness of it. I think some of them get off on knowing that they are the first to whack off to that particular tape. I don't think they care about being the only one, but there does seem to be something about being the first one. "Don't rent it to anybody else," they'll scream into the phone, "I'm on my way!"

Every week or two, there's a new title in the gay section that everyone wants, and we'll start getting calls for it days ahead of time. People call, they beg, they bitch, they try to put it on the reserve list for days in a row. We do our best. The thing is, the movie is hot for two weeks and then forget it – only the poor stragglers who missed the first round want it and then it slowly fades away. It seems simple to figure out that if you just held off for a few days and got yourself a week or two behind the cycle, you could rent the almost-new-but-no-longer-hot releases at your leisure and without all the heartache, but that's not what people want. They want the newest.

I sometimes wonder if it's something akin to the virginity thing or if my renters are, deep down, just as creeped out by some of their fellow renters as I am. If so, I wish they'd think about that for a minute before turning in a spooged out tape that's still stopped in the middle at the exact spot where they came.

Anyway, Mr. Hazy seems to be more about the novelty than the firstness. New Porn Day is actually the easiest day to deal with Mr. Hazy, because as long as he's getting six new videos he's happy. When he's really selecting videos, we have to be careful. Mr. Hazy has terrible eyesight and can't actually read the tags, so he doesn't always know what he's renting. He just finds a box that he likes and pulls the tag hanging underneath.

Usually that's fine, but our customers, as a rule, do not hold degrees in library science. They'll pick up handfuls of tags and then just stick them back under any old movie, or they'll wander around with boxes in their hands, deep in Porn Trance. As a new box catches their eyes, they'll pick it up and put the old box in its place, leaving us with a daisy chain of misplaced boxes to untangle. We catch and fix stuff as best we can, but we're only human. Mr. Hazy doesn't check the title on the tag against the title on the box because he can't, so sometimes what he has is just a random collection of movies for us to pull.

Porn hits a childlike, needy place in many (if not most) of our renters. They were promised a treat and they want it now and if it's already been given away to one of the other kids or not quite the right flavor, some of the guys look like they're going to burst right into tears. Mr. Hazy doesn't look like he's going to cry, but he gets really, really pissed if one of his six(!) rentals for the evening turns out to be the wrong one, and he can really make a stink.

Complicating the problem is the fact that we have several regulars who try to take dirtbag advantage of the fact that we don't make customers pay for incorrect videos. Suddenly we'll see a sudden upswing in a customer getting the "wrong" videos and it's time to put a note on the guy's account and double-check every single frigging thing he checks out every single time so he knows we're on to him.

Mr. Hazy was the first customer I blew my cool with – the only one who's really gotten me angry enough to show it, actually. He'd already come in several times on my watch and turned in the "wrong" movies and this time he said that something like four of the six were wrong and he shouldn't have to pay for them and on top of that he started yelling at me for whoever had so screwed up his rental.

I pointed out that he had a suspiciously high incident of "clerk mistakes" and he slipped and said he hadn't done that in weeks and it ended with me putting each new tape in his face and saying "Is this the correct tape?" before slamming it onto the counter. My fellow clerk Jonathan, who knew that I don't drink or smoke, suggested I take a break and have a beer and a cigarette.

Casey later theorized that Mr. Hazy simply couldn't read, which made me go easier on him and try to feel more charitable, though by then we were sworn enemies.

Actually, as I said, he's simply visually impaired and too vain – or something – to wear his eyeglasses. Which is an interesting lesson in vanity, I think. He didn't want us to know he needs glasses, so one of us assumed he was a lying cheating dirtbag and another assumed he was illiterate. If he'd just said he had sight problems in the first place, we'd have put a note on his file and given him all the extra help he needed. Now we know, and we do.

Store Meeting

We had a staff meeting this Monday night. Meetings start, of course, after we close, which is 11 p.m. This one went until 1:30 (we get time and a half and pizza. Whee!) and of course I was Tuesday morning's opener.

The meeting actually went very well. It's a good, fun crew right now so everyone was pretty cheerful about it, and it looks like we might actually get a workable DVD storage system.

I just thought I'd mention it because we spent a good 15 minutes discussing how publicly a guy has to be masturbating before we can bust him. Obviously, if he whips it out we call the police. Hands down the front of his sweatpants is at least a visit from the Voice of God mic, and a call to the police if we feel like it. (Almost all whackers wear sweatpants. Some of the clerks argue that it's a symptom of having given up on the rules of society, but I think it's simply the easy access.)

Then we got into grayer areas. Specifically, guys who masturbate through their pockets. The evening shift is being plagued by a regular who gropes himself through his khakis. We actually had a discussion on how actively a guy's hand has to be in his pocket before we should bust him. We decided on a quick blast from the call button, which makes a piercing beep, or a pointed "Everything OK down there?" on the Voice of God mic just to let him know we're keeping an eye on him.

I can't believe we actually spent that much time and energy giving the benefit of the doubt to jerkers. I can't believe we're all actually working from a position of not embarrassing these guys. I don't want to embarrass the pocket-whackers either, but why? We all know the rules.

So just as a quick refresher, I'll mention this: While it is perfectly healthy to touch yourself in the privacy of your own home, with special friends, or in special clubs that I don't want to know about so please for the love of God do not e-mail me about them, IT IS NEVER, EVER OKAY TO MASTURBATE IN PUBLIC.

Also it would be nice if you wouldn't crumple up trash and stuff it under our computer monitors.

Thank you.

Instant Karma

I had a pretty good morning this morning. I'm in the good swing of my porn emotional sine wave, where everything is hilarious instead of depressing. Actually, it's not quite a sine wave – I spend a fair amount of time in numb flat-lining mode where nothing even registers. And there are exceptions: *There's a Black Man in My Wife's Ass!* always breaks me up no matter how bad a day I'm having. (Not all the titles can always do that. On bad days, *Whose Pussy Is This?* is a faintly disturbing illustration of sexual domination politics, since I know the proper answer is a breathy "It's yours!" rather than "It's mine, dickhead!" On good days, though, it's a particularly entertaining glimpse into the Lost and Found office.)

Thursdays are usually quiet, and today was definitely slow-paced, but I did have a pretty good stream of semi-regulars.

Mr. Moustache came in with another short stack of porn. I feel bad for Mr. Moustache, and I'm not sure if I should (or could) intervene. He's one of the guys who, I'm guessing, rents porn because he has a little trouble with finding actual women. In my experience most, though by no means all, porn renters fall into one of four major types:

1. Dippers
Dippers by definition aren't regulars. They stop by once to pick up stuff for a party, maybe again six months later when they're a little drunk after a Cubs game. Either they

don't watch much porn or they get it off the Internet. Either way, I don't see them much.

2. Normal, Healthy Porn Renters

These make up the vast majority of my renters. They come in a little more often than the dippers, but not so much that it seems to be making up a major part of their lives. NHPRs may or may not be married or dating someone – the porn is an occasional supplement to a normal sex life.

3. Substituters

These are the guys, both straight and gay, who appear to be renting porn in lieu of having sex with other people. Sometimes it's due to a reclusive or difficult personality, sometimes to, uh, nontraditionally handsome looks. Obviously I can only make an educated guess as to whether someone is an NHPR or a substituter, but sometimes I feel like I'm making a damn good guess. It's usually based on rental frequency, the attitude of the guy returning the tapes (substituters tend to be the most defensive) and a few other personal cues.

4. Addicts

Yup, addicts. Anyone who routinely spends six or more hours a day watching porn. Yes, it's an arbitrary number, but I think I'm being pretty reasonable. We're talking about a third of their waking lives here. Sure, there are grey areas and extenuating circumstances. That doesn't mean there aren't also addicts.

Anyway, Mr. Moustache seems to be a substituter. The thing is, he seems to be an OK guy. I think the only reason he's in the position of substituting is that the moustache in question is a huge, revolting 70's porn moustache. It's just terrible. I'm not sure what effect he thinks he's pulling off, but that can't be it. I wish I could just tell him – if he dropped the 'stache I'm pretty sure he'd do a little better with the ladies. But he clearly likes his moustache and it's not my place and, hell, as it is he's a good customer.

My next regular to come in was Mr. Smooth. Mr. Smooth always, always hits on me. He says one or two generally friendly things, works in either a compliment or an attempt at a double entendre, then asks what time I get off work or assures me that he'll see me later or any other traditional post-hitting-on parting remark. He always glances at me over his shoulder as he walks away and gives me the sly, smug smile of a man who has just done very well for himself.

Today there was a note on his file from one of the other female clerks about how he always hits on her. I was relieved that I wasn't the only one receiving Mr. Smooth's attention, but I'll admit I was also faintly disappointed at the discovery that I have no special allure. Ah, well.

Mr. God came in a little later. He wouldn't be a particularly distinctive renter if it weren't for the huge button he always wears, which I think is homemade:

GOD IS.
IN FULL CONTROL

I am fascinated by the quirky punctuation and always wonder if it was intentional and, if so, what that means.

Mr. God always rents hardcore porn, and it's hard to keep myself from having a knee-jerk snotty internal reaction to that. If he's so pious, why is he renting *Freaks, Hos and Flows*? Which would be a good point on my part if it weren't so hypocritical. One of my beefs with traditional Christianity is that most sects treat sex as a dirty or sinful thing. I like the fact that say, Taoism, treats sex as not only good but sacred. Why the hell can't God be. In full control and enjoy a little porn? I should fully support that. But still, my initial reaction is always a superior internal snort at the juxtaposition of the button with a bag full of *Up and Cummers*. Maybe I should get some sort of shock collar.

Mr. Diamond came in later, and I had a revelation. Mr. Diamond likes to rent the new releases upstairs in the general release section. He never has a new release in mind, he always just asks what's new and then wants to know what they're about. He always comes to the counter and asks what the new releases are even though they're posted on a sign, and he always asks me to show him which boxes those are even though, of course, the titles are on the boxes. Well, a lot of people don't like to find things for themselves and he usually comes in when it's pretty quiet, so it's not really a problem. It wasn't until *Zoolander* was released a few months ago that I realized he couldn't keep up with me when I pointed to the new releases too quickly and, more tellingly, when looking for *Zoolander*, Mr. Diamond hadn't seemed to notice the giant row of bright green and white boxes that said "*Zoolander*" across the front.

Mr. Diamond could not read.

I became a model clerkly compassion. I did my best to help him out without letting him know that I'd twigged to his secret. I put a discreet note on his file so the other clerks would help him out and avoid recommending new releases with subtitles. I admired the fact that he covered so well, that he'd risen to the point of being able to afford his diamond without being able to read. I wondered what his life was like and was quietly proud of myself for being such a terrific person as to help him without embarrassing him.

Anyway, I'm an idiot, because today while I went back to the counter to help with a printer jam he read a box perfectly well on his own. Turns out he doesn't like to use his glasses either. I can't believe I've done that twice now. Anyway, his new releases were all checked out, so I suggested *Lantana* and sent him on his way. I hope he likes it; it'll make me feel better.

It occurs to me that this entry's title actually fits my own comeuppance for being so smug about what a swell gal I was being to Mr. Diamond scant days after reminiscing over my literacy/myopia mistake with Mr. Hazy, but I'd actually intended it for another incident.

A man came in today and a note popped up on his file: "This charmer shoved his tapes on the counter in front of the disabled guy who wasn't getting out of his way fast enough."

The man is screwed for life at our store and he doesn't even know it. No, we won't be deliberately mean to him or shortchange him or anything like that. But we also won't cut him a break on late fees or give him the benefit of the doubt on damage claims or go out of our way to help him out, which we frequently do for people.

Clerk Karma happens more for our customers than people think, and it's odd how far-reaching, if minor, the effects can be. Even the highest management will take a note into an account. A fee on an account with a note that says, "This guy admits it was his fault but he was really cool about it," usually gets reduced by the Powers that Be. "This guy screamed at me for 20 minutes." is unlikely to get the same friendly reprieve.

I like it. We're not penalizing the jerks so much as rewarding the good, and it's comforting to know that life sometimes works that way, even if it's on a small scale. And of course, many small scales I don't know about may be adding up all over town.

We help people out as often as we doom them. A simple "Good guy" or "She's really nice" can invisibly smooth a customer's rental paths for months to come, even if it just means a succession of especially friendly clerks.

I wonder if our customers ever think about the fact that the hand that helps balance out the scales of the universe may have just landed in a wad of their semen.

Out of Context

My friend Joe used to be a counselor. He wasn't a psychiatrist, but the counseling was of that nature – sometimes pretty heavy stuff. One of the rules was that if he saw one of the people he was working with out on the street, he wasn't allowed to show recognition unless they greeted him first. It was a small city and being greeted by the counselor could mean that suddenly everybody knew you had problems.

I sometimes feel like that. Our store is very much a neighborhood store, and I see my regulars out all the time. I try not to recognize them until they acknowledge me. I used to automatically smile and say hi and most people were fine with that, but it did make a few people uncomfortable.

I saw two regulars out of the store last week. Monday was the most startling: I was heading to my theater for a show and suddenly Mr. Buddy leaned out the window of the restaurant next door. It took everything I had to keep from doing a take. I said hi and hotfooted it on my way without telling him where I was going. Mr. Buddy is harmless, but for some reason the thought of him seeing my show weirded me out to no end.

Over the weekend I ran into Mr. Dreadlocks. We'd come to the same peace march. I hadn't seen Mr. Dreadlocks in months – he finally did something weird or upsetting enough that the general manager cancelled his account. (I don't know what, and I feel like if I hit the point where I care enough to ask I've crossed an important line.) I didn't end up talking to Mr. Dreadlocks. We'd always gotten along just fine, but in this case I didn't know what to say. I didn't know why he'd had his account cancelled or under what circumstances he was asked not to come back; a cheerful howyadoin might not have been appropriate.

It's hard not to wonder. Sure, he was creepy, but we have plenty of creepy people in the store. If creepy got you cancelled, we'd be out of business. I'm guessing by the way he fetishized the tapes it was either a lube or tampering issue.

On the other hand, he was really, really into charging small amounts on his American Express card. Three or more $3.69 rentals a day, charged separately an hour or two apart from each other. This was a pain in the ass for the store – credit card transactions under $10.00 can actually lose us money – and we couldn't figure out if it was just a side effect of the fetish or if he was trying to work some angle or what.

At any rate, Mr. Dreadlocks, already a little bit crazy and a little bit sleazy, did something crazy or sleazy or maybe just irritating enough that he can't rent our movies anymore.

He was ahead of me in the march, so I couldn't read the sign he was carrying for a while. My group was a little faster paced than his, and during the course of the march we passed him. I couldn't resist – I had to glance over my shoulder and see his sign.

It was yellow and plastic, with blue cursive writing. It was a sign advertising another, completely different event. For the summer of 2000.

I think I'm going to miss him.

No More Ms. Nice Gal.

Arrrrggghhh.

I was having a lovely morning, right up until the end. Tuesday openers are very slow and I've grown to like them. I get my checklist of clerkly tasks done early and then, except for a very occasional customer, the morning is pretty much mine. It's not a bad way to ease into the day.

Today was going just swell. A little cleaning, a little introspection, and all quiet except for a regular or two.

He came in around 9:30. He was a big guy, dressed in baggy clothes, and he looked like he was either going to ask for an application or how you get a membership. (Correct on membership.) Lots of people come in wearing baggy clothes looking like they're going to ask for an application or a membership, and most of them do. What made this guy distinctive was his hair.

I'll go ahead and admit right off, I am not a fan of white-boy dreadlocks. Someone else can make the arguments about whether it's appropriating or appreciating someone else's culture; I just think they look silly.

This guy had gone one better: He had made an attempt at white-boy cornrows, but apparently hadn't felt like waiting for his hair to grow out long enough to do the braiding. Instead he'd had it cut very short, then shaved little trenches in it. It was an interesting solution, but not an effective one. From far away it looked like he might maybe have something like cornrows if I squinted, but once he got within ten feet of me it was just sort of sad.

The requirements for membership were a little stringent for him, so he said he'd look around while he thought about it. He looked around downstairs for a while, then left.

He came back about an hour later and headed straight downstairs. Someone who leaves and then comes back like that is almost always in league with Satan, so I glued myself to the monitor.

Something was up. He was pacing around, looking at boxes, checking out the cameras (though not as thoroughly as he might have) and in general becoming the living embodiment of the word "furtive".

He started tugging at his shirt.

I didn't know if he was going to whack off or stuff a box under it, but I didn't much care: I was not having it. Tony the beat cop had stopped in to say hi and check up a little earlier, so I knew he must be on the block. I gave him a call and asked him to stop by. I figured Tony doing a quick sweep would be enough to clear the guy out.

Seconds later, I put in a slightly more urgent call to Tony: The whacking had begun.

I had had enough. Normally I'll give someone a call on the Voice of God mic and tell them to cool it, but screw that – the guy was beating off in my store. Fuck him.

Tony agreed. He said to call 911 and not let Bad Hair know anything was up. Done deal.

It felt weird to call 911 about a masturbator – I had visions of fires and floods and children in danger being put on hold as I said "Yeah, I have a clear view of him on the security camera..." and thought about how not an emergency the situation was.

But 911 did not mind. I gave the dispatcher a description of the guy and our store location again and she said that police were already on the block and on their way.

A bizarre, disgusting race was now underway – would the police get there before he finished?

Bad Hair whacked away, then looked over his shoulder. Jesus, was he finished or had he been disturbed?

He started upstairs. Fuck! I came around the counter so I could follow him out and show the police which way he'd gone.

Bad Hair started for the front door – Damn it! – and actually lit up a cigarette as he went. Now there's an "Alive with Pleasure" ad.

Fuck, he'd hit the front door. I charged forward to catch up and see if he was going to duck into an alleyway... and then the firm, disgusted hand of the law landed on his shoulder. Tony and two other officers had made it just in time.

"This him, Ali?"

"Yeah," I said, "I've got him on tape."

And then the Bad Man with Bad Hair was shoved (not so hard as to cause injury, but firmly enough to be satisfying) up against the outside of the store and cuffed while the officers did a very effective combination of questioning and shaming.

Then they took him away.

I signed a complaint, pulled the security tape, and said hell yes I'd show up for any court date they wanted to give me. Vengeful? Perhaps. But it was also very satisfying.

As effective as the Voice of God mic is at sending whackers skittering back upstairs, I have had enough. Why should I let them get away with masturbating in public, or for that matter almost get away with it and think that they can come back later and try it again?

Jesus, public masturbation is a taboo you learn about when you're four years old – how do these grown adult fuckos drop it so easily? I have more respect for the dirtbags who try to steal boxes. At least they're planning to go jerk themselves in private.

There's a piece of equipment in our storage area. I'm fascinated with it because printed across the base are the words "IMPULSE SEALER". It is, of course, for sealing off items that have been newly shrink-wrapped, but lately I've been pretending it's not and it has become an increasingly large part of my behind-the-counter fantasy life. There are many, many people who need to have their impulses sealed, and for some reason they all end up at my store.

No more warnings. From now on whackers will be referred directly to the police.

Staff Meeting

We've had an interesting development. I knew one was coming because a sign appeared at the store this weekend to the effect that all four locations would be closing early Wednesday for a special meeting.

This would be the Wednesday in question, or at least it was when the meeting started.

We all knew something was up because meetings are usually held on a store-by-store basis. Nobody could ever remember having a giant summit meeting before.

No one would tell us anything. Well, actually the manager and assistant manager of our branch told us that they hated the fact that they couldn't tell us anything, and they thought it was a suckola way to do business. They were correct.

It always amazes me when upper power echelons in a company tell staff that something's up but they can't know what yet and then are shocked – Shocked! – when rumors start flying. Well, what did they think? You can't play "I've got a secret" and expect people to cheerfully play along when you have the power to fire them. If there's no information coming down from above, the plebes will use their best guesses to create information of their own.

In this case, it was a Big Deal that had Lots of Points to Work out and yeah, yeah, nothing could be said until everyone was absolutely sure, and I understand that.

That said, I hope management understands why rumors were flying. I was remarkably successful, minutes before the meeting, in maliciously spreading the rumor that we had a new dress code involving orange jumpsuits.

Anyway, to make a long story short, Bob sold the store.

He sold it to a chain, sort of, though not to one of the big ones. I'm glad about that. It's a company that owns several small chains like ours, and also some weird stuff like shoe stores and tanning salons. We'll be keeping our name and, fortunately, our branch managers, but the central managers will be gone.

We're told that day-to-day operations and things like in-store music and our utter lack of a dress code will stay the same, but I'm going to maintain a gentle but healthy skepticism until I see it.

The new administrative managers – ours is named Gary – seemed fine, and remarkably calm given the facts that they'd only found out about their new jobs about an hour before and were now being stared down by about fifty clerks with creative hair.

So we'll see.

But at least for now, I am still not fired.

I Seek the Keymaster

We all used to be masters of our own keys to the store. The thing about having the flexibility of hours that we did (and, for the time being, do) is that anyone could end up opening or closing on any given day. It ends up being a pain in the ass if someone doesn't have a key, so pretty much everyone who's been trustworthy for a month or two gets one. (I got one after a couple of weeks. I think it was the occasion of my first flush of video clerk pride, rapidly followed by my first wave of fear that I might be a career video clerk.)

That is no longer the case. We'd been having some occasional problems with the burglar alarm going off overnight so Nick, the new owner, had Gary, the new whatever-he-is, change the locks. Nick then went out of town and Gary said that we would "discuss" who got keys when Nick got back.

Nick and Gary are apparently used to working with full-timers (everyone on our staff is part-time except the managers) and actually thought they could narrow the key thing down to two openers and two closers at most. Right. Between college schedules, holiday/semester breaks, and the various bands, improv groups and other assorted performances people are involved in, I'm amazed that the schedule gets made at all every week, let alone a schedule that can make sure that one of only four keys is always on hand.

Gary is not great at the scheduling. We just got our first one and many clerks are pissed. I'm not pissed, but it is an odd schedule. People didn't get the hours or shifts they were used to, and a few people have been scheduled for shifts they specifically said they could not work. But again, scheduling looks like a nightmare task. Maybe Gary will get the hang of it. If he doesn't, it certainly won't be for lack of helpful, pointed clerkly suggestions.

I feel sort of bad for Gary. He's been dropped into this situation and immediately had to make a hugely unpopular move. We're annoyed because it seems like the new ownership doesn't trust us, because nobody mentioned to the managers that their keys wouldn't be working anymore, and because until Nick gets back we have to wait for goddamn Gary to show up before we can open or close the store.

Friday morning I spent half an hour waiting on the sidewalk in front of the store. This one wasn't Gary's fault – there was some sort of traffic tie-up – but it was still hard not to be absolutely murderous by the time he got there.

I had made a resolution to reserve judgment on the ownership change and try to be friendly to Gary, but by the time I had spent a full 30 minutes meditating on the fact that if I'd had my own key I'd have been warm, on-schedule to open, and not so fully occupied with trying to find the spot on the sidewalk with the least amount of pigeon shit, I'll admit that I had fallen down a bit in my self-imposed task. By the time he jogged up and asked if I'd been waiting long I gave him a look so full of steaming hot death that he pretty much gave up on chatting. I felt bad, but not bad enough to make polite employee banter.

He was less late on Saturday, but still late enough to eat into my set-up time. I dislike having to rush my store set-up, and I dislike having to wait outside with my early-morning porn customers even more. When I hit the lock in the morning they stream towards the door from all directions, so I know that even the ones who haven't been out on the sidewalk with me have been waiting and watching me stand there helplessly in my own private Beckett tribute.

But we had yet another meeting this week and I think Gary is beginning to see our point on the key issue. We'll see.

We're all hedging our bets. I think we'd like it if things settled into a nice routine and we could keep our jobs but maybe have a more regular schedule of pay raises, but I don't think anyone really believes that. There have been a lot of classified sections of various papers lying around the store lately.

My first interview is this week.

I Miss Mr. Cheekbones

I haven't seen Mr. Cheekbones in months. Casey and I got to talking about him the other day and we both feel bad about it. I'd even had a twinge when I noticed that we'd sold off his favorite video. It was called *Pee for Me*.

Mr. Cheekbones was another customer whose name I learned early on. He usually came in with his headphones on and bopped as he walked around the store, singing along to the music in an odd falsetto range of his raspy voice. He liked porn – particularly peeing-for-each-other porn – and always asked when we were going to get some new kung fu movies, but really his tastes went across the board. He liked to try a little bit of everything, and was just as likely to rent *Othello* or the latest art house release as his trusty, much-rented favorite.

That made him unusual, but that wasn't why I learned his name early on: Mr. Cheekbones was a pain in the ass who I magically turned into a regular.

Mr. Cheekbones liked to prepay for his movies, which we usually don't do. It's not a huge deal, but it does require a special entry in the register and printing out a receipt to put in your drop at the end of the night. Now I could do it while blindfolded, shackled, and under the influence of a horse tranquilizer, but when I first started clerking prepayments were a pain. The prepayment itself bugged me, and then the fact that Mr. Cheekbones always mentioned his prepayment just after I'd checked out his movies and cleared my screen bugged me too. I'd have to ask for his account number again and it threw off my rhythm and now it seems like a very petty thing to be irritated with at all, but I think when I started I was an angrier clerk, or at least a more resentful one. (I wonder if that means I've learned an important life lesson or if I've simply given myself over to despair.)

So I'd get annoyed when I'd see Mr. Cheekbones coming and he'd sense my distaste and be annoyed right back. We didn't like each other, and we kept not liking each other for a week or two.

Then one night he bopped up to the counter and chose David's register instead of mine. David was an even newer clerk than I was, so I gave him a friendly warning.

"That's Mr. Cheekbones," I said, "He likes to prepay."

And suddenly Mr. Cheekbones broke into a huge grin. He was a regular. I knew his face, his name and his preferences. A regular.

After that, we were buddies. We joked at the register, and talked, however briefly, about movies. One night he was checking out new tapes and I told him that the tapes he'd checked out before were due that day. He raced home, swearing he'd be back before we closed. I said he was never going to make it, but he stunned us all by doing it. He made it back to the store, sweating and wheeling his bike, with just minutes to spare. I clapped when I saw him coming.

He also had a pride about the way he paid: bills, not change. Once – only once – he had to pay for a movie with a handful of quarters and dimes, and he was furious with himself. It wasn't a big deal – we don't mind taking change for a $2.10 charge – but he kept saying, over and over, "You know me. I don't pay with change. You know me. I'm not the kind of guy who pays with change." He never did again, or at least not with me.

But we'd been seeing less and less of him for a while, and he wasn't looking too good. He didn't bop, he didn't chat, and he leaned on the counter like he was exhausted.

Once he came in with an awfully small dressing over a wound. Casey and I both thought it looked like he'd been shot. We're no experts, but still.

I don't know what happened, but somewhere in there he got his account cancelled. There's an outstanding charge of about $180 on his account, which usually means someone checked out movies and never brought them back.

Somewhere in there his life took a slide, and I hope he can make it back.

Wherever he is, I hope he has his headphones on.

My Day in Court

This is my own fault. I slacked off on updating (general business and some actual freelance work came up) and now I have to write about the many things that have happened with the curse of perspective. I'll try to stave it off as best I can.

Thursday the 14th was my court date for the whacker. We had to be there a little before 9:00. Megan, my manager, was nice enough to pick me up and drive me there. I hadn't had quite enough sleep the night before and I barreled out of the apartment having remembered to do everything but eat breakfast, so I nearly wept for joy when I discovered that Megan had also been nice enough to pick me up some orange juice and a blueberry muffin. Empathy: the hallmark of an excellent manager.

We actually had a pretty good time. Megan had a mix CD playing, and while we must forever agree to disagree on the joys of Aqua, she did have some excellent non-dance Swedish music. We were a little early, so we chatted, caught up on the paper, and listened to the song that she used to torture her customers with back in her clerking days. It was impressive.

Security tape in hand, we went through the metal detectors (People, for chrissakes. We all know the drill now. We're going to be having our metals detected for quite some time to come. Have your goddamned keys and your goddamned change and your goddamned giant metal belt buckles OFF YOUR PERSON AND READY TO PUT IN

THE LITTLE BASKET. Must we really act like it's a surprise every time? I would ordinarily have been willing to cut people slack on that point, assuming that perhaps they are unfamiliar with airports or courthouses or are from foreign lands where people aren't quite so jumpy about being blown up [Are there any of those left?], but my friend Sheila the lawyer says that she used to routinely watch people be surprised about having their metals detected before court in the morning and then, coming back from their lunch break, be surprised all over again. I realize that in a way that must be a nice way to live, but for the sake of the rest of us, PLEASE WAKE UP.) and found our courtroom.

Our courtroom was the one for misdemeanors and it was packed to the gills. Megan and I only got seats when we explained to the bailiff who was trying to throw us out that we were actually involved in a case and not just hanging out.

The seats were a mixed blessing. We had a good view and reasonable physical comfort, but we also had someone in the very near vicinity who smelled a lot like stale urine. No, a *lot* like stale urine. I was very attentive during our time in court, but there was a renegade part of my brain that would not stop trying to figure out who it was. I had it narrowed down to either the woman on my left or the guy in front of me, but afterwards Megan definitively said it was the guy on her right. Though I was happy to have the mystery solved, I was vaguely horrified to realize that the woman on my left and the guy in front of me may well have had their suspects narrowed down to me.

9 a.m. hit, the judge arrived, and suddenly we were whipping through cases like nobody's business. Megan and I were out of there by 9:30, and there were easily 15 cases in front of us. Most of them were dismissed because the accusers hadn't shown up. Bang, dismissed.

I couldn't believe it at first, but then I realized it was pretty efficient. Clear out the chaff so that the people who are serious about it get more time from the court system down the road. (Marshall Field's, we noticed, does not fuck around when it comes to shoplifting. They had a guy stationed there whose whole job seemed to be showing up as the accuser.)

A couple of people pled out, a few more no-shows, the woman on my left (who, for the record, did not smell like pee) asked to wait a few minutes because her lawyer had stepped out and not come back, and then there was a minidrama: three teenaged boys had their case (Trespassing? Harrassment? I can't remember.) dismissed because their (female) accuser hadn't shown up, but the judge ordered them to all stay the hell away from her anyway.

I was mulling over whether the accuser had been afraid to show up or if hijinks had just gotten out of hand and she didn't really want to press charges or what when the whacker's name was called.

Megan and I went up, but the whacker was nowhere to be found. I wasn't too surprised: his address on the police report was in Michigan and I hadn't seen him in the courtroom and it was, let's face it, a pretty humiliating charge.

The D.A. seemed pretty happy that someone who wasn't just a paid store representative had actually shown up. He put a warrant out on the whacker, told us it might be a while before we heard anything, and off we went.

Megan and I agreed that it had been an extremely interesting morning and wondered if they'd ever actually catch him. I was just delighted to have been on the clock for it.

The New Overlords Are Neither Merciful Nor Just

I had this Monday off.

I walked in on Tuesday morning to find that Megan had been fired.

Well, technically she'd been "downsized," but the net effect was still the same.

It was incredibly weird – she'd put up one last note about busting holiday shoplifters before getting the news, and then she was gone.

Jeremy, once our assistant manager, is now the manager. He's a good guy and will handle it very well, but it isn't the way he'd wanted to get promoted.

Megan, by the way, will be fine. She's a writer and this might just be the shove from Fate that she needs to get going on the life she really wants. On the other hand, she'd been at the store for four years and had worked her way up from clerking. It would have been nice if the New Masters had taken that into consideration.

My understanding is that Megan, having been given a bunch of new responsibilities what with upper management gone and all, had asked for some more money. Instead she was told that we'd be getting a new software system that would eliminate many of her duties and she would no longer be needed.

The decision came from Nick, the new owner, so nobody can quite decide how to treat Gary. Gary has been friendly but extremely and understandably nervous all week.

More changes are, reportedly, on the way.

The new software system will usher in a new way of doing things. Some of them, like the addition of a drop box, will make our customers happy, but I don't think most of them will.

We will no longer allow customers to take IOUs, and we will no longer allow customers to sign up for memberships without a credit card.

In other words, we will be doing our best to prune off our customers with lower incomes.

The credit card thing is especially harsh. I do realize that the ones who sign up without cards are statistically a little more likely to be a problem down the road, but I always liked the fact that we didn't tar everyone who didn't have a credit card with that same brush.

We have people come in from all over town, incredibly far away in some cases, because we're the only store that will give them a membership. Most of them are good customers. What are they supposed to do now?

Even though it means that most of our bigger pains will be eliminated, most of the clerks don't like it, and we're all fairly shaken about Megan getting yanked, and yanked so suddenly.

I spent much of Tuesday ratting out the Overlords to our customers and indeed, I'm continuing to do so.

It's been a weird, sad week. More to come.

I Am Still Not Fired

…But I did quit.

I'd been looking for work for a while. As freelancing work gradually dwindled I was getting more and more dependent on my video store income, which just wasn't cutting it. One of the main reasons I'd been staying at the store was the flexibility that allowed me to take on freelance assignments, which was starting to lose its point. The New Store Order wasn't helping matters either. One of the other main reasons I'd been staying was a fondness for my managers (one down) and fellow clerks, who were starting to do some nervous looking around. The pleasures of working for a funky little neighborhood store looked to be hurtling towards an end as well.

There were more prosaic hardships too. The New Overlords let the general managers go when they took over. In addition to being swell guys, the general managers ordered the store supplies. Suddenly we were doing without incidentals like fresh punch cards and crucial necessities like toilet paper and hand sanitizer. Jeremy would have been more than capable of running out and picking up a few things until supply lines were back in place had the Overlords not also taken away the petty cash. The shift when the sanitizer ran out reduced David and me to jittery wrecks. So many matinee specials came in that day… Eugh.

So, yeah, it was increasingly time to go, if indeed it hadn't been long before.

It had been a long time since I'd had a truly humiliating job search.

The phase when my freelancing started drying up was quietly terrifying, but not actually humiliating. A few freelancing agencies told me they loved my stuff but didn't have any work, a few restaurants giggled at the bartender who was hoping to keep a standing performance commitment every Friday and Saturday night. I signed on with a temp agency (also with a caution that there wasn't much work to be had in the New Economy), but the recruiter was a friend and so it was a painless process. As was my first temp assignment, until Gordon the Friendly Middle-Aged Guy turned into Gordon the Creepy Middle-Aged Guy Who Was Really Into Swinging and Wouldn't I Like to Meet His Wife? As Gordon ignored increasingly less polite forms of "no," suddenly the "Employment Opportunities Within" sign at my local video store seemed like not such a bad idea. (Say what you will about the video store, but not even the scariest porn freak there ever hit on me as relentlessly as Gordon did. Even dirtbags know to take no for an answer.)

But while all of that was bizarre, none of it was actually humiliating. My last big stupid job search was when I'd first moved to Chicago at 22. It was then that it really hit home for me that companies with shitty jobs to offer will do everything in their power to let you know that while there is still dignity in all work, it is not for lack of trying on their part.

I interviewed at a Sheraton that didn't have an HR office, they had a "casting office." I went to one of those massive Tuesday-only application days that hotels have and saw a hallway full of people scrambling for terrible jobs to try to feed their families. They were, according to the application, aspiring "cast members" for the big fun show that is changing dirty linens at the Sheraton. Jesus.

I was young and bright-eyed back then, but in recent years I'd been working for some pretty cool places and then working for myself, so I was out of practice with sucking it up.

I was just called in for an "interview" for a job being a concierge in an office building, which unlike being a real concierge seemed to mostly involve saying hello and occasionally buzzing people up. Instead of talking to someone, I filled out a colossal application that included an essay section on what teamwork (or as they repeatedly and incorrectly put it throughout the application, "Teamwork") meant to me. I had to write an essay on why I wanted the job and how I would throw myself into it in a unique and exciting manner. I had to do a worksheet (even more incorrectly headed "Check Off Which Ones Are Important To You So You Will Give One Hundred Per Cent!!!") in which I checked off "Teamwork," but left, say, "Gossip" blank.

I made it almost all the way through like a good toadie, but then on the last page I snapped. I was supposed to write an essay on what I hoped to achieve at the company over the next several years, but instead I flipped out and got honest on them. I even started the essay with "I'll be honest with you…" I said that the company was not a part of my personal goals, and that, while I would throw myself into any job to the best of my abilities, it would still only be my day job. The advantage in hiring me, I said, was that they would have a cheerfully overqualified employee for maybe the next year or two.

For some reason I haven't heard back.

I'd also applied for a job in the exciting world of telephone reception, to which I am no stranger – it's what I did most summers during college. Reception is incredibly boring and also fraught with rude people, but at least one can pass the time by practicing Sultry Receptionist voices and putting the truly vile on hold for minutes at a time. I didn't really want the receptionist job, but I was really looking forward to the simple joy of knowing where rent was coming from every month. I had an interview – a real one, this time, scheduled for Friday.

And then on Thursday morning I woke up to a phone call. Kurt, the man on the other end, wanted to know if I would like to take over writing and producing an online game for Jellyvision, the software company I used to work for.

Yes, please.

Suddenly bang, a job, and one that I actually wanted. I start Monday after Thanksgiving and I'm looking forward to it: The work will be challenging and fun, the people I'll be working with are terrific, and I dimly remember health insurance being a pretty nice thing. (In a perverse way, I've realized that I'm actually looking forward to my next illness or injury, just for the sheer joy of going straight to the doctor instead of waiting for five weeks to see if whatever it is clears up.)

Everything else happened suddenly too, so suddenly that I never knew Thursday would be my last shift. I thought I'd get one final shift in there Monday or Tuesday to say my goodbyes, and even dropped a note asking for one, but Gary just went ahead and took me off the schedule.

It makes sense, I guess – this way I don't spill over into another payroll week, but still. I dropped by Saturday to find out when I'd be working my last shift and instead turned in my hard-won key. I spent a little time reassuring a pissed-off Casey that I'd never meant to just split without telling anyone, and then it was time to go. I'd always visualized a sort of Dorothy-leaving-Oz moment, but it was the shift change and they were busy and a new clerk had already sprung up to take my place. So we said so long and that was it.

I felt a little bad that I didn't get to spend a last shift cheerfully announcing my departure to my regulars and positively beaming at my dirtbags, and a little sad that I didn't get to thank Mr. Gentle for being such a bright spot, but in the end clean breaks are usually best.

I am no longer a porn clerk.

Addendum:
When people e-mailed me about this journal, hands-down the most responses were about the special joys of Aqua.

But the individual person who inspired the most mail was Mr. Gentle.

I was sad that I didn't get to say goodbye to him. I did get one of the clerks to let me go into the system one last time and leave a note on his file: "Please tell him Ali says thank you for being such a bright spot in her mornings."

As I typed the note, I of course had his contact information right there, but to use it would have been a violation in a couple of senses, not to mention way too creepy. And I wasn't really sure what I'd say.

So I had to leave it.

He found out I'd left when the other clerks rolled out the red carpet for him once they saw the note. Anyone who had dealt with him before already liked him, but that definitely gave him a little extra oomph.

He, as it turned out, asked for my contact information, but, to their credit, no one at the store would give it to him. He understood.

One clerk did, however, tell him about this blog, and a few days later I got an e-mail from Kevin Mullaney at the Improv Resource Center that finally put us in touch.

And then a day or two after that we ran into each other on the street, which undercut the drama of the search a little bit, but was still fun.

I think the first thing he said after hello was "I'm royalty at the store now!"

Mr. Gentle and I became close friends. We still are.

So if I were to give one last piece of wisdom I picked up at the video store, it's to trust the hunch that you and that person might get along really well.

Let's Talk Evolution

As soon as I started clerking (or, rather, as soon as I started telling people that I was clerking) people wanted to talk to me about porn.

Sometimes it was with the same combination of giggle and frisson that is normally used for bringing up a silly-yet-scary ghost story, sometimes it was with an almost scientific detachment, sometimes it was with prurient interest, and sometimes it was just because the over-the-top world of porn is frequently hilarious. Actually, it was usually a combination of all of those. I'm not being superior when I mention that – I dove into the conversations before I got all cold and dead to porn, and I'll admit to getting quite a bit of mileage out of my odd little job at more than one cocktail party.

Anyway, almost all of these conversations ended up with the other person at some point saying something like this: Men like porn because they are evolutionarily programmed to sleep around and make lots of babies with as many women as possible. Women don't like porn because they need to catch a man to provide for her babies and keep him forever and ever.

In other words, men are bad, but they just can't help it if they screw around. Women don't get to sleep around, but isn't it nice to be inherently virtuous?

Because, I think, I politely resisted saying this in every single case, I'm going to take the liberty of doing so now: That argument is complete horseshit.

Evolutionary success is not about having the most sex, it's about producing the most fertile offspring.

To rephrase: The idea isn't to spread the most baby batter around, it's to raise the most children who themselves grow up to produce children. That's why your parents won't leave you the hell alone about making them grandparents; their jobs aren't done until you do.

If you're just spreading sperm around, you're not strategizing your evolutionary success well at all.

Male sleeping around simply wouldn't have cut it as an evolutionary strategy. First off, the male in question can't just sleep with any old female for evolutionary success, he has to have sex with a woman who is currently fertile.

Human females have concealed ovulation. Fucking around means rolling the dice each time, while staying with one woman at least through a full cycle (or two, or three – our ancestors didn't have our ridiculous abundance of food and thus weren't as reliably fertile) meant a good shot at pregnancy.

...And that's assuming that the opportunity for Cro-Magnon or australopithecine fucking around existed at all.

Illicit sex requires privacy, and the days before bricks, mortar and loud stereos didn't provide much. Ever try to get away with something in a small town? Now try it when you live in a community of 60 breeding adults who live in thatched huts around a central campfire. Everybody knows your business.

And there's not a lot of stealing away for you-time when there's a danger of being eaten by predators. Doing things alone, for that very reason, tends to be looked on with suspicion when it happens in pre-modern societies, to the extent that it happens at all.

I once read an account of an anthropologist's attempts just to go out to urinate without company. The people he was living with couldn't figure out why he'd want to do such a dangerous thing.

I'm not saying that affairs never happened back in the mists of time, just that they would have been damn sight harder to have than we think of them.

And while a single fling might have been possible if dangerous to attempt, being a rake would have been out of the question. Again, in a small community, word gets around. There aren't many evolutionary advantages in being ostracized by your clan or getting your head caved in.

Even if someone did manage to buck incalculably high odds and impregnate more than woman (and assuming the women don't abandon the offspring), he still has an evolutionary problem – the kids have to reach adulthood and have kids of their own.

His time and provisions would be split between more than one mate and more than one child, decreasing the odds of anyone getting enough food or growing up completely healthy.

The "faithful" male only has one child at a time, but can devote his whole energy to making sure the pregnancy goes well and both mother and child are healthy and well provisioned. You have better odds raising well-fed children with two sides of a family for support than scrambling to split food between multiple children, some of whom may bear a stigma from having no socially sanctioned dad and only half the number of clan members helping out.

The healthy kids with family backing them up are more likely to have a prime choice of mates, and thus more likely to have healthy children of their own. Over thousands of years, it adds up.

On the other hand, women have more of an evolutionary reason to screw around than you'd think.

Theoretically, a woman who can overcome the (still huge) odds, have an affair, and convince two (or more) men that they've fathered her child can raise her child with the advantages of extra provisions and extra adults looking out for it for its entire life. Again, healthier growth, better choice of mates, more surviving offspring in the long run.

My point is that men are not evolutionarily hard-wired to screw around and never commit and women are not biologically "meant" to pick just one. There are (or at least were) advantages to both in being faithful, and advantages and dangers to both in screwing around.

The men-get-to-sleep-around-and-women-stay-home thing isn't in the evolutionary hardware, it's just deeply embedded in our culture.

Saying that women are naturally good girls and men can't help being dogs is a cop-out for both genders.

It gives men an excuse to do a lot of unexamined sleeping around and women a way to pretend that they never have stray naughty thoughts about sleeping with the entire tuckpointing crew that's working across the street.

It's easier for men to just go on cruise control and not make the effort of being faithful (and thus vulnerable) to one person.

It's easier for women to just coast along being nice girls and not dealing with the fact that temptations are very much there and look like a hell of a lot of fun. Or that the anxiety over settling down may have more behind it than pure, inherent virtue.

Watching several men rent hardcore video after hardcore video over the past year and a half has solidified this position for me.

The ones who rent four or five or six a day, the ones who call on New Porn Day and want to reserve the new ones and paw through the boxes and then can't wait for the next New Porn Day seem to be looking for something that mere variety can't give them. Maybe it's trite, but sometimes I can't help but wonder if slowing down and taking the time, risk and effort of dealing with one other human being for a bit could show them a glimpse of that thing.

On the other hand, when women wrinkle their nose at tales of my workday, I sometimes wonder if pawing through the boxes until they found an image they liked might be just the thing they were looking for as well.

Valedictory Address

Writing this journal has taught me many things.

The first is that people who hold a given point of view too passionately tend not to be careful readers.

I've had rabidly anti-porn people (mostly women) tear into me because I didn't say that all porn ever is inherently evil, and I've had ferociously pro-porn people (mostly men) send me frothingly outraged e-mails because I didn't say that all porn ever is healthy, free, and wonderful.

Both groups almost invariably accused me of writing things I hadn't – and sometimes accused me of taking positions when I'd clearly written the opposite sentiment. At first I thought I was being willfully misinterpreted, but then I realized that these people were just seeing what they expected to see, and what, I think, they wanted to see. It's hard to deal with someone's gray areas when you're spoiling for a fight.

But that has been the only negative. Mostly this odd little burst of pseudo-semi-almost-fame has taught me that people are funny, thoughtful and kindhearted.

I was amazed at how many strangers dropped me a note to say that they'd enjoyed something I'd written or just to say hang in there and it would all be over soon. I couldn't believe how many people who were brand new to the IRC message boards kicked in a donation to keep them going when the bandwidth got tight.

As for the old IRC hands, I knew they were a nice bunch, but I've been constantly floored by their generosity of spirit. Performers and writers are supposed to be viciously jealous and competitive, but these have failed miserably at that. Their eerie ability to drop notes of praise and support just when I needed them made me much bolder about sending around writing samples, even ones without porn in them. Thanks so much for that.

While I'm at it, I'd like to say thanks to everyone, past and present, at my video store. I am forced to agree with Mr. Buddy: you rule.

To everyone else, I'd just like to say this: Be nice to your video clerks. Rewind, take your late fees like an adult, and keep the spooge to a minimum. Better yet, be nice to anyone you meet in a customer service position. Odds are very, very good that they're having a rougher day than you are, and it's easy to become a store favorite just by being The Friendly Guy Who Never Yells.

And, in the immortal words of Aqua, be HAPPY!

Love,

Ali

CPSIA information can be obtained at www.ICGtesting.com
Printed in the USA
LVOW06203421081

295324LV00001B/170/P